10 Principles of
Good Interior Design

10 Principles of Good Interior Design

Vinny Lee

VIVAYS PUBLISHING

Published by Vivays Publishing
www.vivays-publishing.com

© 2011 Vinny Lee

A catalogue record for this book is available from the British Library

ISBN 978-908126-10-8

Publishing Director: Lee Ripley
Design: Keith Lovegrove
Cover Design: Andrew Shoolbred

Printed in China

PREVIOUS PAGE
Streamlined monochrome kitchen with central island work station and white painted floorboards.

COVER
Photographer:DarrenChung/ Mainstreamimages/the-englishstudio.com

RESERVED

POP ART

Introduction

Good design achieves
a sense of place

Introduction

Deciding how to decorate your home can be a daunting task, some people look for inspiration in the pages of magazines, or the colours of a favourite painting, even the pattern of a carpet or curtain fabric. Then there are the tricky questions of how to find an overall style? What shape of furniture to choose and how to arrange it so that the layout of the room is comfortable and cosy but still spacious and easy to move around? All these things make it difficult to know where to start.

There are tricks of the trade and all sorts of information available on websites and through designers and decorators, but the aim of this book is to simplify and structure the ten basic principles of design so that they are clear and easy to follow, whether you are starting a scheme from scratch or reinventing an existing space.

As you gather ideas it is helpful to put them in a file or folder, especially pages taken from magazines showing the particular drape of curtain or piece of furniture that you like, plus swatches of paint colours or fabric that might work in your decoration plan. Also have a specific note pad in which to keep useful phone numbers, colour references and lists that you can tick or amend as you progress.

By following the guidelines outlined in the subsequent chapters you will be able to create a scheme that has depth and interest as well as expressing something of your personality which is important because individuality is what turns an apartment or house into a home.

Good design achieves a sense of place, somewhere with an interesting and memorable appearance. This can be done by highlighting architectural features, using colour cleverly and the careful arrangement of furnishings and accessories. As with fashionable clothing the most successful 'looks' are achieved by mixing and matching brands and labels, as well as things that are old and new.

A complete, head to toe designer outfit will be memorable for the designer label rather than the person wearing it, but if you customise the outfit with your own accessories and mix in a

ABOVE
When creating a decorating scheme a mixture of textures, colours and patterns will make the room a more interesting and enjoyable place.

FACING PAGE
The arrangement of furniture in a room is important, it can be used to frame or highlight a feature but it should not obstruct or hinder the free flow of movement through the space.

LEFT
Artwork doesn't have to be static, move it around from time to time for a different focus or emphasis on an area, and vary the shapes and sizes of frames.

FACING PAGE
Extending a doorway upwards can create the impression of added height in a room and instead of a single door, two narrow panels can also look more interesting and elegant.

different shirt or belt, then the outfit will take on your look rather than that of the designer. The same applies when decorating a room, it is how you interpret and adapt a scheme that makes it unique to you.

Don't be intimidated by the vast array of choices and the mass of information available. It is a matter of editing it down until you find what suits you, and remember you don't need to be wildly bold to make an impact, subtle shades, simple furnishings and a few well placed accessories can be effective when creating a comfortable and relaxing home.

ABOVE
By facing the doors of this walk-through wardrobe with mirror the light from the bathroom is reflected making the inner, windowless space bright and interesting.

FACING PAGE
Architectural features such as a decorative cornice or a period fireplace can inspire a decorative scheme and add character to a room.

Purpose and Function

Evaluate your space

PRINCIPLE 1

Purpose and Function

One of the first rules of design is to make a room fit its purpose, so begin by evaluating the space you have and work out how it can be best used.

When looking at a room, whether large or small, it is important to decide exactly what it needs to do. Ask yourself some basic questions, for example will it be a primary function space with just one task, such as a shower room or a dual function space with two tasks such as a kitchen dining room?

Part of this analysis involves looking at your lifestyle - if you don't enjoy cooking and entertaining at home then you won't need a large kitchen so you may be able to free up space to accommodate another task such as laundry, or if you have a lot of possessions or equipment, additional storage.

Conversely, if the kitchen is small but you want to use it for dining and entertaining as well as cooking, could functions such as the storage required for a pantry/larder or washing machine/dryer be relocated to another area therefore freeing up space to accommodate a table and chairs? Would a folding table be an option, so that it can be stored away neatly when not required?

If you have a busy family home with adults and teenagers rushing to get out of the house at the same time, an additional lavatory or shower room could relieve the pressure on the main bathroom. The shower or lavatory could be installed in an unused or under-used space such as beneath the sloping rise of a staircase or in a bedroom where an enclosure could be constructed or a bath slotted in behind a low or half wall or an opaque glass screen.

The direction a room faces will affect the penetration and quality of natural light and may also influence your choice of what function you place there. For example a bedroom that faces in the direction of the sunrise will be light and bright in the mornings making it easier to wake up and get out of bed, whereas a room that faces in the opposite direction will be cool and dark first thing and make you want to stay under the bedclothes.

This sort of analysis and overview will make you think about each room in turn and explore the options and possibilities available.

ABOVE
A corridor or passageway can be adapted to provide a study area for homework or a home office; here ample natural light makes it an ideal location for a desk.

FACING PAGE
A mezzanine or split level can be built within a tall room to reduce the ceiling height and provide useful extra living space.

In this linear room the sofa has been placed along the wall opposite the window so that those sitting on it can enjoy the view and natural light. The fireplace is on an angled wall which faces into the room and provides a focal point.

ROOM BY ROOM

Living Rooms

A living room has two main aspects, it is generally regarded as the most 'public' or sociable space in a home because it is where strangers as well as friends and family will be greeted and entertained, but it is also a place for rest and relaxation when you are on your own.

In this room it is useful to combine 'fixed' and flexible furniture. There could be a large sofa that would be difficult to move, but provides seating for several people or a place for a couple to lounge, as well as a couple of light weight individual chairs that can be arranged against a wall when not needed but brought in to the room when required.

The area where you watch TV or films could be located away from the windows, in the darker inner area of the room because direct sunlight will reflect off the screen and make it more difficult to watch. But a comfortable seat for reading, or a study area or desk will benefit from being by a window where there will be direct access to natural light.

ABOVE
Open plan, linear rooms can be difficult to furnish, here the sitting and reading area has been put close to the window for access to natural light, whereas the dining area, used mostly in the evening, is in the darker, centre section of the room.

FACING PAGE
A study area may be created in a small or awkward space, even under the sloping roof of an attic. Because little head height is required above a chair, this seat can be neatly fitted below the low section of ceiling.

Kitchens and Dining Areas

The practical elements of a kitchen will put restrictions on its location and on the way the layout can be arranged because you will need direct access to water and waste outlets which are usually ducted through an external wall. The type of surfaces you can use will also be dictated by requirements such as heat resistance and hygiene, and in a room that contains both kitchen and a dining area good ventilation will be essential to remove steam, heat and cooking smells. So these aspects need to be factored in to the layout at the earliest stage.

In kitchen design there is a format known as the 'work triangle' which, if followed, makes ergonomically efficient use of the space and minimizes the amount of walking between the three main functions of food gathering, food preparation and cooking. If you place the points of the triangle too far apart you will add to the amount of walking you do each time you prepare a meal and if the points are too close your kitchen will be a cramped and an uncomfortable place in which to work.

The three point of the triangle are the sink, the refrigerator and the hob and/or oven. It is advised that each leg of the triangle is

LEFT
In this corridor two columns of shelves and storage baskets have been positioned on either side of the radiator which also has a bench constructed in front so that people can stop here to put on or take off shoes and outdoor clothes.

FACING PAGE
A bench seat with storage drawer underneath has been fitted in at the end of a unit in this kitchen, creating an informal seating area.

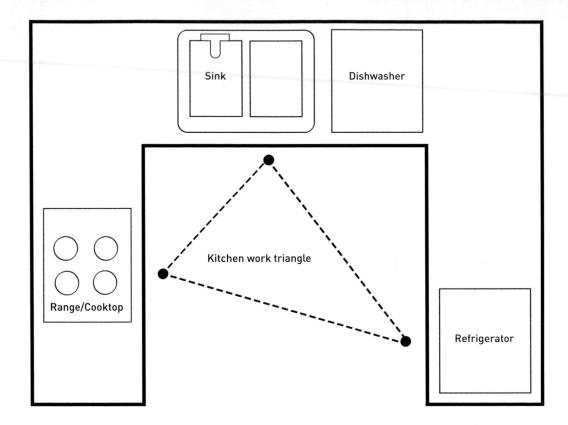

Sink

Dishwasher

Kitchen work triangle

Range/Cooktop

Refrigerator

between 4 feet (1.21 metres) and 9 feet (2.74 metres) apart, depending on the size of your room. The total distance between all three legs should be between 12 feet (3.65 metres) and 26 feet (7.92 metres) and the space within the triangle should not be on the main thoroughfare or obstructed in anyway.

An island unit or breakfast bar is a popular way of providing extra work surface, storage and an informal dining area; it may also be used to create a barrier between the areas of cooking and more formal eating. Island units can be square or oblong, and currently popular are mobile islands that have locking wheels so that the island can be moved around a room to cater for different functions such as a buffet table or bar, or pushed closer in to the kitchen area to make the dining section more spacious.

Halls and Stairs

Our experience of a place is strongly influenced by how we arrive in it – as the expression goes 'first impressions last the longest'-- so an entrance hall or lobby is the place to make a statement, to set the scene.

Entrance halls often have to contend with a number of roles, not just being the point of arrival and departure but also the place where outdoor clothes are put on and taken off, boots and shoes are stored, mail arrives and even as a parking space for bicycles and skate boards. If your hallway is such a place you should provide adequate, efficient storage and keep the decoration simple because the things kept there will be take up visual space and the background should not compete with them.

In older homes, stairways and hallways tend to be without much natural light so you will need to factor in well-positioned electric lighting so as to avoid accidents and also to make it easy to locate things.

In many contemporary homes staircases are designed to double as light wells so that daylight from a skylight or large window on the upper level shines down through the stairwell. It may be possible to replicate this feature in an older home too by installing a Perspex dome or Velux window into the roof.

Another way of bringing in light to a hallway or stairwell is to replace solid panels on a staircase with fine balustrades or reinforced glass. High tension wire may also be used, but you will need to check what is approved by your local planning authorities.

If you have a spacious hallway or landing you could create a study with a desk and shelves or a children's games/play space, or build in box seats that provide a quiet reading area with useful storage underneath.

ABOVE
Well positioned lightIng, interesting artwork and a bright decorative scheme can turn a dull windowless corridor into an appealing location.

FACING PAGE
Reinforced glass panels can provide adequate safety on a staircase without blocking the view or flow of light, here a decorative light feature emphasises the rise of the stairs.

EXPERT ADVICE

Karen Howes owner/founder of Taylor Howes Designs, award winning international interior designers www.thdesigns.co.uk

" Understanding purpose and function is the first step in designing a home. It is essential to know how someone will live in and use the space, and then to introduce ideas and concepts that fulfil but also challenge the way they think about things. Clients are used to seeing their home in a certain way but, as designers, we come in with a fresh eye.

First we create a floor plan with key pieces of furniture drawn in place, this helps us to visualise how the clients use the space, then we go to the next stage of placing lighting, heating, audio visual, storage etc.

At Taylor Howes we like to create glamorous but practical interiors and I often say that we know more about our clients than anyone else, what side of the bed they sleep on, how many pairs of shoes and handbags they own, how they like to entertain, where they watch television, and whether they like to bathe or shower – all these elements need to be taken into account when creating a successful and comfortable home. Without purpose and function you will never be able to create a truly great interior scheme – the secret is to make it effortless. "

Bedrooms

The bedroom is a sanctuary, a private space where we go to relax and sleep so the layout and design of this room should encourage and support those aspects. Although clothes storage is an important factor, in many bedrooms the main concern is usually the positioning of the bed that is often influenced by the location of the window and door.

Few people like to sleep directly under a window because it can be cold and draughty. If there is any view, it is more pleasant to lie in bed and look out at it rather than have it behind you, so a bed is usually positioned facing or to the side of a window. The door opening in to the room should ideally be to the side of the bed rather than directly in front of it, so as to screen the bed from the direct view of the corridor.

For ease of access you should also be able to walk unhindered around both sides and the foot of the bed, enabling you to get in and out of it easily especially in the night. Most bed heads are pushed up against a wall, although in some large rooms the bed can be positioned in the centre of the room.

Many bedrooms contain wardrobes; these can be built-in or freestanding. If you plan to build in wardrobes, do take into

consideration the room required to open the doors. If space is restricted you may need sliding or concertinaed doors. If you are in a shared flat or a home where there is a busy corridor outside your bedroom, you may want to put the wardrobes against the wall facing the corridor because the furniture and clothing inside will provide a certain amount of sound insulation. And if you have a cold, north facing wall in your bedroom a wardrobe built along that side can be used to provide extra heat insulation.

Instead of putting wardrobes in your bedroom you could create a walk-in wardrobe behind a false wall. To do this you would need to section off part of the room with a light, stud wall, reducing the overall size of the bedroom but creating a separate and easier access to hanging and clothes storage space.

Other furniture that needs to be taken into consideration when planning the layout of a bedroom are bedside tables, chairs and a chest of drawers, all useful pieces that will add to the comfort and easy use of the room. But if space is restricted bedside tables could be built into the headboard or could be lightweight and shelf-like, secured directly to the wall.

ABOVE
By raising the bed on a tall custom-built base extra storage has been created in this compact bedroom and, to make getting into bed easier, a small step has been added at the foot.

FACING PAGE
The positioning of the bed is an important when creating a comfortable bedroom; try to keep a free flow of space around the bed so that it is easy to get in and out.

Sometimes it is possible to double up functions, for example in a large bedroom a bathroom or bathing area may incorporated, but it is important to have adequate ventilation to avoid moisture building up and damaging the fabrics in the room.

Bathrooms

Bathrooms have similar restrictions and requirements to kitchens and hallways. As with kitchens, the water inlet and waste outlet will influence where the lavatory, basin and bath can be located and surfaces need to be water resistant and easy to clean. As with hallways, bathrooms tend to be windowless, internal spaces so it is essential to make the most of any available light and to create an attractive ambience using artificial light.

In many homes people choose to have more than one bathing space, often having a separate shower room with a shower and a bathroom with a bath. The shower is used for quick daily bathing whereas the bath is for more leisurely relaxation. Shower rooms

ABOVE
In households where a couple get ready at the same time, having two hand basins can save time and stress. Here tongue and groove panelling adds a period feel and protects the lower half of the wall from water splashes and spills.

FACING PAGE
Wet rooms are a great way of fitting a shower in to a restricted space, but they need to be fully tanked or lined with a gently sloping floor that drains all the water to a central outlet.

can be created in relatively small spaces and with sliding or folding doors, don't require much room to get in and out of. These days baths come in a range of sizes so that a small but deep bath can be installed with a shower overhead, making it possible to put a bathroom in a limited amount of space.

There are also ranges of macerator lavatories that don't require direct access to mains outlets. These 'light use' facilities can provide a useful option in a family home or one built on many levels.

ABOVE
The curving wall on which the lavatory and basin are hung, ekes out extra millimetres of space to create a viable extra shower room.

FACING PAGE
By angling the bath from the corner in to the room, rather than flat against the wall, extra space has been found and the bathroom also has a more memorable and distinctive appearance.

PRINCIPLE 2

Style

Find a look and stay true to it

PRINCIPLE 2

Style

Style is defined as 'giving cohesion and meaning to a collection of objects'. This can be done by thoughtful grouping and arranging, and in selecting a colour or theme that unites and brings the various pieces of furniture and fabrics together.

Choosing a style of decoration for a room may be influenced by many things; the love of a colour or place, by the date the building in which your home is located or the design and period of the furniture you have. You may prefer not to have any dominant or definitive theme, but instead devise a layout and colour palette that brings together a variety of elements. The main thing to remember is: find a look with which you feel comfortable and stay true to it.

PERIOD STYLES

The historical period in which a building was designed and constructed can give you a direct link to a style of decoration fashionable at that time, to the furniture that was made to be used in the room and the fabrics that would have been appropriate. But within each period there are a number of variations.

For example in the British Victorian period there were various fashions and phases such as the Gothic Revival, with rich fabrics and decorative ceramics; the Arts and Crafts Movement pioneered by William Morris; French Style with ornate decoration and gilding and the Classical Revival inspired by archaeological digs and discoveries by Victorian travellers who ventured to Egypt, Greece and Italy. So that within each era there is considerable choice.

Each period style also has its own range of colours, these were influenced by the type of pigment or dye stuff available at the time, but now many paint manufacturers offer the contemporary equivalent in ready mixed ranges, for example The National Trust have a range of paints specifically catalogued according to historical period.

Wallpapers from various eras are also widely available, William Morris designs are still printed by Sanderson and classic Regency stripes are manufactured by many companies, so finding a paper that fits a particular style era is feasible.

When you have established an appropriate colour palette

ABOVE
A simple fret-cut decorative arch can give an instant Eastern feel to a room and the shape of the arch echoes that of the bed head.

FACING PAGE
Some styles evolve from a mix of ideas and influences, here a tribal feathered hat, classic marble topped console and kelim covered cushions are brought together by a strong but muted palette of colours.

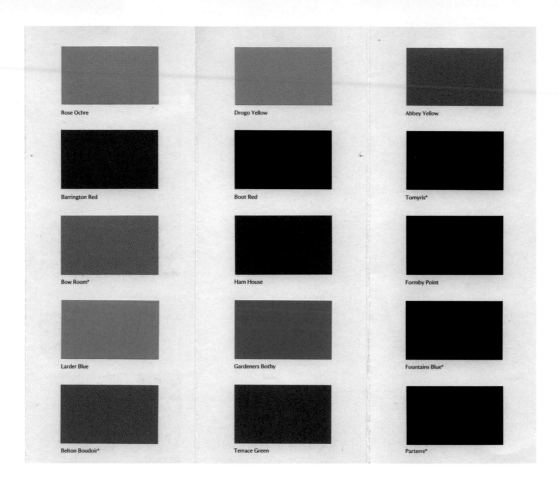

Rose Ochre

Drogo Yellow

Abbey Yellow

Barrington Red

Boot Red

Tomyris*

Bow Room*

Ham House

Formby Point

Larder Blue

Gardeners Bothy

Fountains Blue*

Belton Boudoir*

Terrace Green

Parterre*

ABOVE
The National Trust Paint Palette is inspired by colours found in old houses and paintings. Many have a direct reference to the past and can be useful when creating a traditional or classic style of interiors.

FACING PAGE
This room has many original features including the ornate plaster cornice, panelled window shutters and intricately patterned parquet wood floor which provide a strong sense of period and style.

(a collection of colours) you will find that it complements the furniture and fabrics of that period and style. Wedgwood Blue, named after the colour of the ceramics produced by Josiah Wedgwood's factory in the mid 1700s, is associated with decoration and furnishings of classical Georgian homes. While Chinese red, taken from the red of the Chinese lacquerware imported during that period was popular with those who decorated their homes with Chinoiserie embroideries and carvings.

The colours of the 1950s have a soft muted hue that works well with the textile prints of the designer Lucienne Day and the furniture of her husband Robin Day. The 1960s palette contains intense and vivid colours such as orange, purple and shocking pinks which set off the moulded plastic furniture and Pop Art patterns of the time. If you choose to follow a specific period style you will need to research the appropriate colours and designs of the time.

Artwork, material or carpet

A style or look can be inspired by a possession, such as a painting or a rug. The colours within the picture or woven pattern can lead to the development of a palette of complimentary and contrasting shades that will accentuate and enhance the object.

For example a modern, brightly coloured abstract painting that is the focal point in the room may look best against a plain white wall, and in keeping with the style of the artwork, contemporary furniture would be appropriate. As the walls of the room are white, the accessories, such as cushions and throws, could be chosen to echo the colours within the painting.

If you have a large decorative rug in the centre of a room you could look at its pattern for potential decorating colours. Where there is a bold pattern in a strong main colour you could look at lighter subtle shades derived from it, or a contrasting colour (see chapter 5 on Colour).

A country or exotic style

Throughout history there has been a fascination with the styles of other countries. China, India and Japan have been popular in several eras, more recently the textiles, ceramics and basketwork of Africa and also Mexico have provided themes for room schemes.

These location inspired styles need to be handled with care so as not to create a room that looks as though it is just stuffed with holiday mementoes. Choose a few good quality objects, and

ABOVE
The colours and abstract composition of the artwork hanging above the bed have been used as a key for the colour scheme and choice of wallpaper in this room.

FACING PAGE
An elegant Biedermeier sofa from a style created in Germany in the early 19th century sits comfortable beside a modern bench table and seat because the wood tones are similar and the rest of the decoration is simple, which also allows the elegant shape of the sofa to be appreciated.

Although this kitchen is at the heart of a contemporary family's home, the style is in keeping with the period of the building. The paint is a chalky based, muted shade; the new oven has a traditional appearance and a reproduction drying rack all contribute to the classic appearance.

Sometimes comfort can be the leading
motivation in a scheme, a big
comfortable sofa on which to lounge,
read or watch a film may be the
starting point from which a decoration
project featuring restful colours may
evolve.

FACING PAGE
A combination of rustic beams and
modern furniture and fittings works
well in the pared-back space.

perhaps one or two appropriate fabrics that can be used in cushion
covers, curtains or a throw, but use sparingly.

Non-specific Style

Rather than focusing on one particular look or period you may
choose to have a mixed or unspecified style, such schemes are
sometimes referred to as 'Classic with a twist' or 'Modern with a
dash' so that the strongest impression given is either Classic or
Modern, but then with a little something extra or different.

When bringing together furniture from a variety of periods and in
differing styles you will need to be careful when selecting fabrics
and wall coverings. Balance the mixed shapes and sizes of the
furniture with simple patterned curtains or blinds and plain or
subtly designed floor coverings so that the overall appearance of
the room is calm and compatible rather than a jumble of patterns,
shapes and colours.

EXPERT ADVICE

Lulu Lytle, founder of Soane Britain, London
www.soane.co.uk and www.soaneantiques.co.uk

❝ No two people will perceive style in the same way and really it is indefinable but I shall try to encapsulate what it means for me. Fundamentally style is instinctive therefore if you are trying, you don't have it and if you are forcing something to work then it probably won't.

Style is individual and instinctive and cannot be bought or taught. It is spontaneous and above all it inspires. It is not confined to the visual and is an approach, a way of doing things. A genuinely stylish person is at ease with how they express themselves be it visually, verbally or emotionally.

On a visual level it can be a very fine line that divides a room that is stylish or not. It may be superficially perfect but is it alive? Does it have soul? I can't be prescriptive about what makes a room stylish, it might be excessive or restrained, elaborate or simple, rigorous or free. It might reveal something about its creator but it doesn't necessarily. What every stylish room does possess is balance and scale. **❞**

Individual style

There are a number of designers and decorators who have created their own style, their 'signature' look and these have gone from being the style of one individual to a look that has become widespread through being copied and replicated.

Amongst these 'signature' designers is the American Elsie de Wolf. She banished the formality and darkness of the Victorian era with a focus on comfort, leopard print fabrics, 'plenty of optimism and white paint' and the mixing period and styles.

Another American, 'Sister' Dorothy Parrish, is credited with creating the American Country Style which features overstuffed armchairs, a variety of patterned fabrics and patchwork quilts. She was famously the first interior designer brought in to decorate the White House during the Kennedy presidency and her work can still be seen in the Yellow Oval Room and the Family Dining Room.

Although these are grand staterooms, Sister Parrish's style for more everyday homes focused on the use of bright colours, in

ABOVE
Painted wooden panelling and a well worn flagstone floor provide the period setting for furniture which is a mix of contemporary and vintage but in sympathetic and classical shapes.

FACING PAGE
In this rustic kitchen the furniture and accessories have been kept simple, from the scrubbed wooden table to the Willow pattern plates and dishes and pheasant feathers on the broad beam mantle above the fire.

particular yellow and what is now known as Shabby Chic. She put together a mix of bric-a-brac and family heirlooms and maintained that design should focus on what people really enjoyed rather than a strict adherence to what matched and co-ordinated.

Contemporary French designer Andrée Putman is associated with a monochrome palette of black and white with chrome, and restrained simplicity. Some say that her style is a contemporary interpretation of Art Deco with a focus on clean crisp lines and geometric shapes. And the Italian Giorgio Armani has become known for his chic but rich style in interior as well as fashion design, featuring stylish and well made pieces in subtle and muted palettes.

There are books about most leading designers, and if you aspire to their style you can look through pages of photographs and highlight the key pieces and features that are crucial to their looks.

ABOVE
A simple palette of brown, cream and blue used in blocks of plain colour and in various widths of stripes gives this room a clean but interesting appearance.

FACING PAGE
The colours in the poster hung on the wall above the sofa are reflected in the tone of the wooden floor, the upholstery material and the pale green chenille cushion.

Space and Shape

There should be a logical flow through a home

PRINCIPLE 3

Space and Shape

There should be a logical flow through a home so that it is an easy and comfortable place to live in. To achieve this you need to analyse the shape and size of the room, the furniture you intend to put in it and how it will be best positioned.

First look at the general layout and arrangement of rooms so that those used in conjunction with each other are grouped together. For example bedrooms and bathrooms are used simultaneously so they should be side by side or even with the bathroom en suite to the bedroom. Kitchen and dining areas can be located in the same or adjacent rooms so that hot food doesn't cool when being taken from the kitchen to where it will be eaten.

These are obvious examples, but in a multi-levelled house you may find it easier to make space for a laundry room on the upper floors near the bedrooms and bathrooms where clothes are taken on and off, rather than in the basement which will make it necessary to walk up and down several flights of stairs with clothes that have to be washed and ironed then brought back upstairs to the bedroom.

In a family home it is often beneficial to put a quiet study space on the upper level and the children's play room in the basement, or vice versa, so that there is a sound barrier of a couple of floors between the two locations. If you do locate a study on an upper floor or in a converted attic space make sure that you have plenty of electrical sockets so that you can have a mini fridge and a kettle point for making tea and coffee.

The flow through a home should be clear both physically and visually, you should feel that you can walk from one side of a room to another without having to tackle an obstacle course of foot stools and side tables, and also when you walk into a room it appears spacious, ordered and inviting.

Once the general layout has been considered, turn your attention to the selection and arrangement of furniture. Remember not to crowd a room with too much furniture or to arrange it too closely together, especially if you are using bold colours or strong patterns. Allow each piece of furniture space 'to breathe' and on a practical note, it will also make it easier to clean the room thoroughly.

ABOVE
A study area and music room have been slotted in to this attic space, skylight windows on either side give access to daylight without disturbing the roofline of the building.

FACING PAGE
By removing the ceiling and opening up in to the rafters you can gain valuable extra head height, although the roof will need to be well insulated to guard against heat loss.

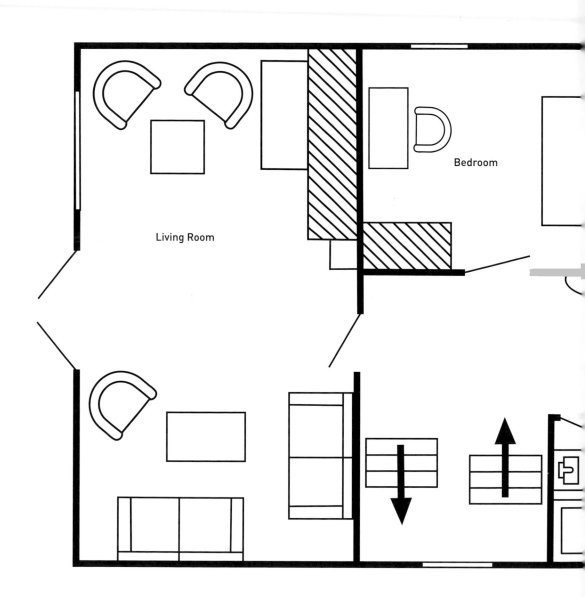

Living Room

Bedroom

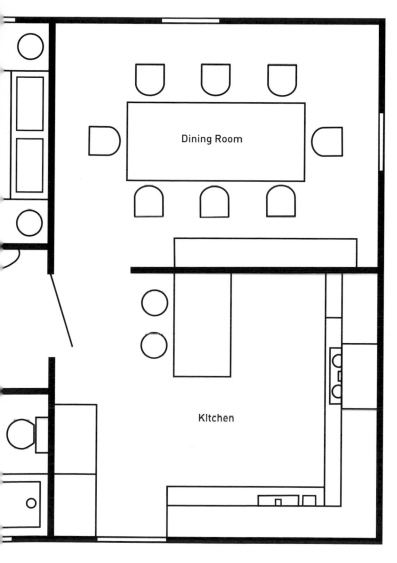

Dining Room

Kitchen

This basic floor plan shows how the through flow of space works in an apartment. All the doors open into rooms easily and no furniture or obstacles obstruct them; you can walk through the apartment from one end to the other without having to veer around footstools, side tables or chairs; the living room has a larger entertaining space with sofas and a chair but also a smaller more intimate space with just two chairs. In the bedroom the bed can be accessed from both sides and is not directly visible from the doorway. There is room for everyone at the dining table to pull out their chairs and walk away from the table without having to disturb another diner. These are all factors that should be considered when planning your space.

A substantial dresser acts as a wall between this dining area and the raised kitchen beyond. In some locations you may not need to actually construct a wall, a large piece of furniture, a bookcase or screen can acts as a room divider.

FACING PAGE
The staircase acts as a visual barrier between the kitchen and dining area and the sitting room beyond. The open treads and sides of the stairs means that light flows easily from one side to the other keeping a feeling of openness and space.

If your room is small, then slim line, lightweight chairs and tables will look best and avoid skirts on chairs, long table cloths and plinths on the bases of cupboards and units because these will make your furniture appear as solid blocks. By allowing the eye to see across the floor, through chair arms and around tables you will create an impression of space.

By laying stripes and lines in certain directions you can also accentuate the feeling of width or length. If you lay floor boards or a striped rug with the lines running lengthwise across a room, the eye will register an impression of length, whereas if you put the stripes running across the width of the room the space will appear wider.

Another way to make maximum use of your space is to angle the furniture. This will sometimes allow you to position a piece that is oversized into a small space. For example, if you want to put a full-size bath into a long narrow room, try positioning it across a corner rather than flat against a wall, you may find that it fits more comfortably at an angle, rather than parallel and squashed up against a hand basin or other bathroom fitting.

Spacious, open plan rooms can accommodate larger more solid

By sinking the bath into a raised floor, the windows and view in this corner space have not been obstructed. The compact but deep bath can also be used as a shower with attachment mounted on the wall between the windows. This clever and economic use of space shows how a luxurious bathroom can be slotted in to a restricted space.

EXPERT ADVICE

Yabu Pushelberg, designers, New York and Toronto
www.yabupushelberg.com

❝ A room that is perfectly symmetrical can impart a sense of serenity, where everything is in balance and each object, work of art and piece of furniture has a strong sense of place. Such a setting feels right; the energy flows unhindered and there is an atmosphere of harmony. Ideally the dimensions of this type of room should be roughly equal so that the ceiling height is similar to the width, and the overall volume of space should be generous and imply a gracious stateliness.

Conversely, an unusual or asymmetrical space will suit a less formal, more casual approach. If the space is for entertaining the furniture layout may be broken down into smaller groups. The main pieces, such as sofa, armchair, coffee and corner tables, may take on a central role. Thereafter smaller seating groups can be placed in other areas of the room. In its own way, the multiple seating groups visually balance the irregular configuration of the room and allows for a more casual flow of socializing and conversation amongst both the resident and their house guests.

This breaking down of the bigger space into smaller rooms within the room can also be enhanced with unusual shaped furniture, furniture of varying seat heights and maybe also a mix of furniture styles. The overall mood should be of free-flowing social hubs within a single space. This manner of approach in itself, suggests another kind of confidence and grace. ❞

pieces of furniture, but it can be difficult to create a feeling of
intimacy and comfort. Some professional designers use rugs or
carpets to visually subdivide the floor and assign a certain area to a
specific function, so that one rug delineates the sitting area,
another the dining area and a third the TV or study space.

Freestanding bookcases and screens can be used to create the
feeling of a room within a room, and low back sofas grouped in a
square will also create the feeling of a contained space. On a more
ambitious scale, a tall room can be divided vertically by making a
mezzanine floor to provide a bedroom, study, home office or media
room and also reduce the feeling of empty space above your head.

Another designer device that can be used to make large
bookcases and solid cupboards appear smaller and less bulky is the
'shadow line'. This is a small recess or gap at the top and bottom of
a unit which makes the eye register space which visually reduces
the impression of volume.

Once you have sorted out the location of rooms and the
arrangement of furniture within them, take a look at the patterns
and colours of the upholstery and curtains, this will be covered in
more depth in chapters 5 and 6, but it is important to factor this in

when looking at the proportions of a room.

There are some simple rules to follow when calculating the proportions of a room, and it can be worked out loosely with a simple equation. For example, if you have a small room and a large sofa, the sofa takes up a third of the room and is therefore going to dominate. If you upholster the sofa in red it will look big and overpowering, however if you cover it in a red and cream check fabric you reduce the volume of red by half because the cream is a neutral and calming shade. Thirdly, if you upholster the sofa in cream but add red cushions and a folded red throw, the red part of the equation is reduced to about a tenth and therefore makes the room appear more spacious and calm.

ABOVE
This low back L-shaped sofa acts as a nominal room divider creating a barrier between the kitchen and sitting spaces, but it does not restrict the flow of light from the windows.

FACING PAGE
Spiral staircases require less space to install than standard rise and tread stairs they offer a neat solution to preserving floor space while accessing an upper floor, but are governed by strict planning regulations.

PRINCIPLE 4
Light

Natural light is free and usually
more restful on the eyes

PRINCIPLE 4

Light

In this chapter we look at the different types of light; ways of 'finding' or 'creating' light with mirrors and back lit panels, also how to use it to 'paint' and create dramatic effects. Good lighting is a flattering accessory in any home, but it is also important for health and safety reasons, to avoid eye strain and to be able to see clearly where you are going.

The way we view a room is affected by the light in which it is seen. A shaft of sunlight will brighten even the darkest space, but it is transient and difficult to control, whereas with electric light you can vary its intensity and direction to create different moods and atmospheres.

Natural light is free and usually the most restful on the eyes so maximising its use is worthwhile. On the downside direct sunlight can cause glare and, in time, may cause the colours of fabrics and furniture to bleach and fade, but this can be controlled to some extent with louver or roller blinds, or light muslin or voile curtains. And in winter, daylight can appear flat and have a bluish or grey hue making some colours appear cool and dull.

In an area where there is little or no natural light, there are ways of amplifying what is available or creating the impression that it is there. For example in a hallway or room with a small window, place a good size mirror opposite the light source to reflect and magnify the light. Painting the surrounds of a window and its sills with white paint will increase the amount of light reflected back into a room, and by tying back curtains so that they frame the edge of the window, rather than hang over it, you will also increase the access of natural light.

There are a wide variety of artificial light sources available from the new generation of LEDs (Light emitting diode) to the more conventional tungsten bulbs. LEDs come in small, delicate bulbs and pliable protected strips which can be positioned under shelves or around curved or arched surfaces, they use a quarter of the amount of electricity required by a fluorescent light and last up to ten times longer.

Electric lights can 'colour' the way we see. For example halogen bulbs give off a bright white that is stimulating and vibrant but isn't

ABOVE
Artificial light can be decorative as well and functional. Here Hollywood style bulbs frame the mirror in a small cloakroom and add an air of glamour.

FACING PAGE
As well as having a folding door and a side window this room benefits from a large glass ceiling panel which allows a flow of daylight into the room and a constantly changing view above the table.

restful or particularly flattering, it may also appear to 'bleach' pale or subtle colours. Tungsten bulbs have a yellow hue which is flattering to colours from the 'warmer' end of the spectrum, but can make shades of blue seem green, therefore it is important to study fabric and paint swatches in both natural and artificial lighting to get a true impression of their colour.

Different types of lights are also suited to specific areas and needs. Task lights, such as the classic Anglepoise, are usually adjustable so that they can be directed on to a work surface or the page of a book for good visual clarity. Accent lighting, as in flood or spotlights, can be used to highlight a painting or feature in a room and these lights often come with shutters or shields so that the beam is directed specifically onto the object being highlighted.

There is also ambient lighting, the general or background light that creates the overall illumination of a space. This category of light includes centre or pendant lights that hang from the ceiling, but in general this is a wash of basic, fairly flat light which needs to be augmented by the other types.

ABOVE
In this basement kitchen and dining area there are several layers of light: recessed down lighters in the ceiling, a row of ceiling lights with decorative shades over the table and in the kitchen task lighting focused on the work surface.

FACING PAGE
The adjustable heads of this floor-standing task light can be angled to suit a number of requirements such as reading while sitting in the chair or highlighting objects on the shelves.

EXPERT ADVICE

Sally Storey of John Cullen Lighting, London
www.johncullenlighting.co.uk

❝ Lighting is a versatile and functional design tool that gives a magical touch to any interior or exterior. It can create illusions of space and volume, define zones in open-plan areas, highlight architectural features and provide intriguing decorative effects.

Successful creative lighting requires a careful balance of different sources of light and an appreciation of the effects that can be achieved through direction and control. To create an exciting and dynamic lighting scheme, it is essential to understand how to achieve a successful balance of what is lit and what remains unlit. Don't be afraid of shadow, but instead have fun manipulating light and playing with how an object is lit to create different effects with silhouette and shadow.

In a well planned scheme, the various lighting effects are built up in layers, so that the room can be lit in different ways to create different moods, depending on the level and quality of light required. The key is not to use all the effects simultaneously or to the same intensity.

Each lighting phase should be controlled separately so that it can be combined at different levels and brought up individually to alter the mood in the room. I love adding drama to a long corridor or walkway which is often forgotten, or decorating an entire wall with light, or using a simple device such as a spotlight focused on a single object. Above all, lighting schemes should be atmospheric and mood enhancing but also practical, hardworking and magical. **❞**

Ceiling lights can be decorative and may reflect the period or style of decoration, for example a sparkling crystal chandelier for a romantic style or a 1950s Noguchi or Henningsen shade would work with a scheme of that era, so in some cases the centre light has a decorative role as well as a practical one.

In modern homes ceiling lights are often halogen spots or down-lighters recessed into the ceiling. Some are static, but others can be directed or positioned to focus or to wash decoratively down the front of a bookcase or cabinet. This type of light is particularly useful in rooms with low ceilings or in areas where head height is restricted.

The positioning of lights will also affect the way the room appears. A floor lamp or up-lighter recessed into the floor, positioned behind a chair or at the foot of a bookcase can be directed so that it projects a beam or wash of light up a wall therefore focusing attention on the cornice or ceiling, and

ABOVE
This cluster of individual lights on rigid poles is like an artwork and is a feature of this bathroom, but the on/off light switch should be outside the room and the installation must be carried out by a professional electrician to comply with safety regulations.

FACING PAGE
A starburst centre light brings colour and excitement to an otherwise monochrome scheme, but as it is a vintage fitting it may have had to be rewired to comply with modern standards.

emphasising the height of the room.

Mid-level lights, such as table lamps, supply illumination for those who are seated, some may have decorative shades and the colour of the shade will influence the strength and clarity of the light. Floor standing, standard and wall mounted lights provide light at a higher level than table or side lights and can be used to increase the intensity of the ambient light. And when the centre or ceiling light is dimmed these table and floor lamps will create a relaxed and comfortable atmosphere and focus attention on the centre or mid-level of the room.

In a room with no windows, such as a bathroom, you may be able to create a fake window on a wall by mounting a panel of opaque or sandblasted glass in a painted wooden frame with a row of low watt lights behind. The opaque glass will help to diffuse the electric light so that it appears to be evenly spread like daylight. But this style of lighting must be professionally installed because of safety regulations and the danger inherent if water and electricity come in contact with each other.

Another area where professional installation is always necessary

ABOVE
Lights recessed into the wall of this staircase and on the shelf behind the banister on the upper level give a decorative spot lit effect to the stairway, but also direct light onto the treads so that they are clearly visible.

FACING PAGE
In this bedroom an adjustable floor light provides illumination for reading as well as a more general light for the room. The natural and artificial light are also magnified by the wall of mirrors at the foot of the bed.

These gracefully arched French doors provide a wash of daylight to this room and rather than hamper their elegant shape with curtains, the original wooden shutters, which fold back into the side panels, may be folded over the windows at night for warmth and privacy.

is in the kitchen, again because of the proximity of water and electricity. In a kitchen you will need specific task lighting to focus on the areas where food preparation takes place. Good lighting is essential to avoid accidents when using a knife, boiling water or heated ovens and hobs.

Light can also be used in a painterly way so that beams are directed to focus attention on a display of art glass, sculpture or a painting. It can also be positioned so that less attractive features are in the shade while attention is drawn to the best features, and in a large room a focus of light on a certain area can create a feeling of intimacy and comfort.

Dimmer switches are an easy way of varying mood. Lights can be full-on for reading or other such activities, but then dimmed for watching television or evening entertaining.

ABOVE
Task lighting is important in a kitchen, here a wash of light reflects off the steel back panels behind the hob and illuminates the gas rings as well as the work surface at the side. Many appliances, such as fridges and freezers come with integral lighting systems.

FACING PAGE
In a windowless bathroom a panel of backlit, opaque glass can create a window like effect, and if you install a range of coloured light options you can change the mood of the room at the flick of a switch.

Lampshades can be a point of interest and again used to accentuate a period or style of design. For example in a room with a pale scheme, three or four richly coloured lampshades on imposing bases will create an impact.

Candles are a decorative form of lighting and should be used with care, but the light they produce is soft and flattering and can be used to focus attention on a table top or fireplace while the rest of the room is illuminated in a dimmed or subdued light. Candle light is particularly good on a table setting or shelf where there is glassware or shiny metal such as gold or silver, because it will reflect and glimmer in the adjacent surface.

ABOVE
By lighting behind this unusually shaped freestanding wall and two individual areas of the stairs, this corner of the room becomes a focal point. The scheme also uses different colours of light – white for the main section and a yellow hue light for the detail features.

FACING PAGE
Instead of having a solid wall between the upper and lower rooms of this house, a low balcony has been constructed, this not only allows heat to rise from the lower room it also allows natural light from the windows and skylight on the upper level to penetrate to the room below.

PRINCIPLE 5
Colour

Colour stimulates us visually
and emotionally

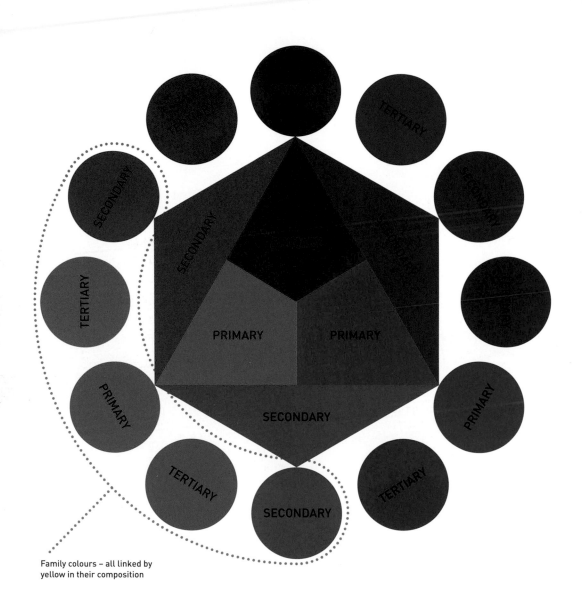

Family colours – all linked by
yellow in their composition

PRINCIPLE 5

Colour

A good understanding of colour is essential when creating an interesting and comfortable home. By putting together your own palette of colours, shades and tones you will establish a feeling of place and give a room a memorable identity.

Colour stimulates us visually and emotionally and its effects are more than decorative; it also plays an important role in the way we feel and respond to our surroundings. Therefore choosing the right colour palette for your room is a fundamental part of creating a home.

You can easily add or subtract colour, it can be introduced in many ways all of which will contribute to the overall scheme from walls and floor coverings to fabrics, furniture, accessories and lights. Colour can be an effective tool when it comes to heightening and accenting certain features or areas of the room and may also be useful in remedial ways, such as changing negative spaces in to positive ones. A coat of white-based primrose yellow paint will transform a dark windowless passageway into a light and inviting hall or the introduction of red-toned colours can make a large cool space feel warmer and more intimate.

There is an art to blending and mixing colours, and science and technology have influenced the ranges and strengths of colours available to us. In historic times colours were obtained from natural substances, such as crushed beetle shells, mineral ores, plant roots, mosses and lichens, but these colours were not fast or durable, they would quickly fade and diminish with use and exposure to sunlight and had a matt rather flat or chalky appearance.

In Europe the blue extracted from the woad plant was used for adornment, often colouring of skin and later for dyeing of textiles. Colour was expensive to produce and therefore particular shades were associated with certain classes and hierarchies. For example in China, the emperor and empress wore yellow, the imperial ladies violet, and noblemen of the first grade blue and in Roman times purple was worn only by the Emperor and senior members of the senate.

Many of the old fabrics, wallpapers, tinted plasters and painted

ABOVE
A bright orange splash-back gives this kitchen instant visual impact and works well with the rich wood units because both share a common yellow and red base.

FACING PAGE
The Colour Wheel shows the three primary colours, red, blue and yellow, the secondary colours purple, green and orange made from equal quantities of two primary colours, and the tertiary colours made up with more of one primary than the other. The bracket on the left groups together a family of colours; this one brackets those which share a proportion of yellow in the composition.

walls that are uncovered in ancient buildings appear pale and subtle, but originally they would have been much stronger and eye-catching. With time the organic based pigments have lost their original strength and power.

From the mid 1800s with the Industrial Revolution and the development of science-based industry, more lasting colours were created. The first modern synthetic dye was invented in London in 1856 by William Perkins who discovered the aniline purple known as Tyrian purple, and later as mauve, in coal tar, a waste product of the coal gasification.

Further developments followed in Germany with the production of artificial alizarin red (in 1869). By early 1900 a new type of coal-tar dye was developed and the chemically based indanthrenes blue, which was colour fast and brighter, replaced the natural dye indigo. In 1956 chemists at Imperial Chemical Industries (ICI) in England announced the first dyes to chemically bond with fabric; these fibre-reactive colorants ensured greater fastness and durability.

There are three main colour groups, Primary, Intermediary or Secondary and Tertiary and each group has its own role to play when creating a decorative scheme.

ABOVE
Many shades of pink and blue are brought together in this room but are balanced by a large proportion of white, both in the wall and ceiling as well as in the fire surround and the cushion designs, so the strength of the colours is diluted.

FACING PAGE
Colour doesn't have to be applied in a solid block, here a wash of paint gives an interesting watery feel to the wall. This can be done by diluting emulsion paint with a little water and applying it with a sponge rather than a brush.

ABOVE
Many shades of pink and blue are brought together in this room but are balanced by a large proportion of white, both in the wall and ceiling as well as in the fire surround and the cushion designs, so the strength of the colours is diluted.

FACING PAGE
Colour doesn't have to be applied in a solid block, here a wash of paint gives an interesting watery feel to the wall. This can be done by diluting emulsion paint with a little water and applying it with a sponge rather than a brush.

PURE AND PRIMARY

Primary colours are vivid and can prove overpowering in a domestic setting unless diluted with plenty of white or neutral shades, they should be used carefully and in moderation:

Red

Red is a hot and emotional colour linked to energy, passion and desire. Historically red has been used in large cold rooms to bring a feeling of warmth. It is also a colour favoured for the walls of galleries such as the Dulwich Picture Gallery and The Royal Academy of Arts in London's Piccadilly. Paintings framed in black or gold and sculpture in white or grey marble are enhanced by a background in this colour. In a hallway or entrance area, where natural light is often limited a red rug or runner is welcoming sight.

Yellow

Yellow is another 'hot' colour so any shade with an element of yellow in its composition will add a feeling of brightness and warmth. Yellow, being the colour of the sun, is said to promote cheerfulness. It is also one of the colours most affected by the light source by which it is seen. A shade of yellow seen in daylight may look bright and fresh but will appear sludgy and dull in artificial light, so test yellow based paints and fabrics in various lights before including them in a scheme.

ABOVE
This bright primrose yellow is a fresh and cheerful colour in a small kitchen; it is also a colour that promotes a feeling of happiness and wellbeing.

FACING PAGE
The contrast of the crimson carpet against the black walls of this stairwell creates a dramatic impression, and the brilliance of the red prevents the black from being gloomy or oppressive.

ABOVE
The bath panel of turquoise-tinted reinforced glass is backlit so that it appears to glow, giving it a different appearance to the surrounding mosaic tiles that are in the same shade.

FACING PAGE
Blue is sometimes thought of as a cold colour, but if the shade has a hint of red in its composition it will appear warmer and more restful.

Blue

Blue is categorised as a cool colour because it reminds people of water and the sky and is said to be calming. At the White House in Washington there is an oval Blue Room where the President of the United States receives guests, the colour presumably calms people before meeting him. Blue should be used with care – too much can create a feeling of coolness especially in the northern hemisphere where the light is less warm and it can be depressive and create a feeling of loneliness.

SECONDARY

Secondary colours are purple, orange and green which are formed by mixing equal quantities of the primaries therefore: blue + red = purple; yellow + red = orange and yellow + blue = green. Secondary colours are often regarded as being more interesting and versatile than the three primaries because they have a more complex composition.

Green

This is the colour of nature and freshness and many of the names given to shades of green are nature inspired such as Apple, Olive, Moss, Pistachio and Forest. The calming and restful aspects of the colour can be seen firsthand in TV studios and theatres where you will often find a Green Room, originally painted green to give actors eyes a rest from the glare of the stage lights, but these days it refers to a room where guests go to relax before going on stage or on air.

Orange

This is an energetic, hot colour but can be moderated if used with a palette based on earthy tones of brown and taupe. Orange is rarely used for a whole scheme, it mostly features as a highlight or accent colour. Orange was popular in the 1960s and 70s in psychedelic and Pop art prints and designs and is often used as a base coat before the application of gold leaf or gold paint, because it gives depth and intensity to the upper layer.

ABOVE
All white kitchens can sometimes appear clinical, a splash of colour will prevent that, a strong colour such as this flame orange works because there is plenty of light, the room is large and the surface is reflective rather than mat.

FACING PAGE
A corridor or passageway can be a good place to inject a blast of strong colour; these areas often have little access to natural light so bright colours work best.

EXPERT ADVICE

Jonathan Adler, potter and designer, New York
www.jonathanadler.com

" So many people shy away from using colour in their
homes for fear of getting it wrong. In a quest for
tastefulness, they take the risk-averse route of avoidance,
acquiescing to perfunctory, pallid hues and a paucity of
pattern. But ignorance and fear are no reason to live in a
bland box. Beige is a bummer! Colourless is
characterless! So vanquish the vanilla: Bold colours will
make you happy! When you're on your deathbed and
about to snuff it, you want to remember the fuchsia sofa.
Colour makes rooms memorable and gives them a mood
like no other design element. **"**

ABOVE
A feature wall of lavender blue makes an impact in an otherwise simply decorated room. This shade is said to be restful and calming so is suitable for a sitting room or bedroom.

FACING PAGE
In this ornately furnished room the impact of the purple wall is lessened because much of it is concealed.

Purple

Purple has the energy of red calmed by the coolness of blue and is said to be a beneficial colour with which to decorate a room where contemplation or meditation takes place.

BLACK AND WHITE

Black and white are technically shades rather than colours, and when used together in their pure forms they create a monochromatic scheme that can be dramatic and sophisticated.

White, whether on a painted wall or as a background in textiles, will lighten a room and appear to brighten the other colours with which it is used. Black is a good contrast because it emphasises and accentuates vivid and bright colours. Black can also be used to create a feeling of perspective and depth and when used as a background makes the area seem to recede, appearing smaller and further away.

When mixed into another colour black will darken and subdue, while white will lighten and brighten. This darkening and lightening of a colour creates what is called a shade or hue and may be used, as part of the same family of colour, to extend the range of a decorative scheme.

Shades of grey can be restful and calming, but should be mixed with brighter highlight colours to prevent the overall appearance from being dull or muddy.

FACING PAGE
This mid-tone grey is used with bright, fresh white ceramics and fabrics in a bathroom and adjacent dressing area. The clinical, clean white offsets any negative impressions that might have been associated with the shade of grey.

GREY

When black and white are mixed together they form grey which, like its components, is a shade rather than a colour and when grey is mixed with another colour it makes it a softer more muted shade (for more information see the next section on Shades and Tones). Grey is popular with contemporary designers and is often found in natural materials or in shades that refer to them by name, for example stone, slate and charcoal.

Grey is a good balance to intense colours such as shocking pink, acid yellow and turquoise and has an affinity with silvery metals such as chrome, silver and steel. You can also have 'warm' and 'cool' greys, the warmer shades being tinged with red while the cooler versions have a hint of blue.

NEUTRALS

Neutrals are undemanding shades that provide a subtle background to bright accessories and richly patterned wallpapers. Neutral colours have names such as oatmeal, magnolia and ecru, chalk and parchment – implying a hint of yellow, pink, beige, grey or blue in their composition. There are also warm and cool neutrals, therefore those with hints of red or yellow or others with a blue base.

ABOVE
The delicately patterned wallpaper gives a wash of warm but neutral colour to this room which is also furnished with oatmeal carpet and upholstery and a darkly contrasting dining table and fire surround.

FACING PAGE
The dark wood floor, leather upholstered sofa and wall panel are lifted by the white ceiling and end wall, the proportion of dark and light colours are equally balanced so neither dominates.

SHADES AND TONES

This is the third or tertiary layer of colour composition which involves tones, the lighter and darker shades of a main colour created by adding white, black or grey. For example by adding white to cobalt blue you would create a pastel blue; by adding grey you create a smoky or dusky blue; by adding pure black you would make a black with a blue undertone.

A family of colours

A family of colour is sometimes referred to as the basic palette which is a range of colours connected by a common base or primary colour. For example, green, orange and brown all share a common yellow 'ancestry' although in different quantities, but this shared base colour makes them compatible.

To extend your palette, or range of colours, you can use the base colour (yellow), family colours (green, orange and brown) and shades (lighter and darker tones) of all those colours. This will give you the flexibility to make a scheme with depth, variety and interest.

Neutral shades provide a good background against which to mix patterns and textures, here delicate voile curtains, appliquéd cushions with surface detail and woven upholstery fabrics share a common colour palette but come together to create an interesting and memorable scheme.

ACCENT COLOURS

In decorating terms the colour used in the largest quantity or in the greatest proportion is classified as the dominant or main colour and the colours used in smaller areas are referred to as subdominant. Accent colours are those that cover a small area but offer a contrast because of their intensity or 'opposition' to the main colour.

Accent colours can be contrasting colours which are found at the opposing side of the colour wheel or spectrum to the main colour. For example, if your palette is predominantly yellow then the opposite or contrast colour will be purple, for blue it is orange and for red the opposite is green. An accent colour may also be a tonal variation, which provides a subtle and sophisticated contrast. For example in a room that is predominantly beige, a single wall or chimney breast of chocolate brown will alleviate the sameness of the scheme.

In a white room any colour can be used as an accent, but make sure that the colour is picked up elsewhere in furniture or accessories otherwise it may look isolated rather than an intended feature. To link the accent colour you may include it in fabrics such as a colour in tweed upholstery or printed textile. The colour may also be carried through in glassware or ceramics and seasonal plants and flowers.

Colour choice is personal; it is about the way a person responds or reacts to colour. Some people feel that pale colours are cool and may make them feel physically chilled, while others find them light and refreshing and, in contrast, a strong deep colour can, for some, be uncomfortable and claustrophobic so the choice of colour is dependent on an individual's reaction.

ABOVE
In this plain white kitchen the accent colour turquoise is used for the splash-back and the seats of the two stools. It is useful to use the accent colour in more than one place so that it looks deliberate and part of the overall scheme.

FACING PAGE
This small shower room is given a punchy and invigorating lift with the use of a panel of coloured, reinforced glass. The shade is picked up again in the vase on the basin surround.

COLOUR IN A ROOM

Living and sitting rooms are often decorated in neutral or off-white shades with furniture, accessories and artworks in stronger or more pure colours; this is because the living room is a shared space and needs to accommodate the taste and requirements of other people.

Another option is the *shared scheme* that is most often found in a family home. This is where different styles and colour preferences are brought together to make a single scheme that is acceptable to the two or more parties who inhabit the space. *Shared palettes* can be complex to devise, but can result in unusual and interesting mixes.

Other people choose to decorate with the *fashionable palette* picking up on colours and trends that are in vogue and seen on the pages of interiors magazines. This is a changeable palette that will need to be regularly updated.

Finally there is the *mixed scheme* where diverse objects, fabrics, furniture and textures are brought together by a common or compatible colour that gives a visual cohesion and unity. For example, a strong colour such as red or black will provide a background to ethnic prints, paintings, wall hangings and artefacts, allowing the colours and patterns of the individual objects to stand out, but not overpower the room.

In a dual purpose room such as a combined kitchen and dining area, you may want to create a visual separation between the two functions, but keep a feeling of unity within the room. This can be done by taking a dominant colour from the kitchen, for example the colour of the unit fronts, and using it as a pale wash of colour on a feature wall in the dining area or as a colour within a pattern or woven fabric cushion cover or cloth.

If your dining room is a separate space, you are free to create a completely different scheme. As it is a room most often used for

ABOVE
Although the scheme of this room is neutral and relaxing, the overall appearance has interest because the paint and fabrics are in a range of tones and hues from the one base colour, brown.

FACING PAGE
In this predominately neutral scheme the single orange chair and vase of Chinese Lantern flowers create an impact. A little strong colour goes a long way.

ABOVE
This bedroom in a rural French house is predominately white, which is cooling and refreshing in the summer heat, but pale covers and surfaces are prone to marks, so if planning to use them for upholstery ensure that they can be easily removed for regular cleaning.

FACING PAGE
The decadent style of this bath has been accentuated by a wall of rich amber tones and the cool metal side of the bath is warmed by the high level of yellow in the scheme.

formal occasions and evening meals, it can be decorated with rich jewel tones that will act as a complementary background to candle light, sparkling glass, silverware and classic white china.

Bedrooms are often decorated in restful and muted tones such as lavender or a subtle shade of peach or Celadon green, but again the choice is down to individual taste and style. There are some dramatic red bedrooms that have a boudoir feel and others in shades of the night such as black, midnight blue and deep purple.

In a home with two or more bathrooms you may choose to decorate one with bright fresh zesty colours for morning washing and showering, and the other with richer more luxurious tones for a lingering scented bath and relaxation. And accessories such as towels and bathmats can also be used to introduce colour. If your scheme is predominantly pale then introduce contrasting or bright towels to create an eye-catching feature.

Colour is something to enjoy, don't be afraid of experimenting, you can always paint just one wall in a light shade and in time paint a darker shade on top, or start with a couple of vibrant cushions and add a darker throw. Take it a little at a time until you feel confident.

ABOVE
This spacious bathroom would look cold and bare if it were decorated solely in white; the addition of rich, yellow based shades keeps it fresh but adds warmth.

FACING PAGE
Blue is the colour of water so it is often used in bathroom decoration. In this small shower room a strong and solid dose of the colour makes creates an impact.

Pattern and Texture

The balance of plain and patterned surfaces is important

PRINCIPLE 6

Pattern and Texture

Colour is a vital part of any decorating scheme, but it is intrinsically linked to pattern and texture. A room decorated in solid blocks of plain colour and flat, matt fabric will look dull whereas a mix of textured carpet, leather upholstery and embroidered and chenille cushions will have interest and variety.

You will find that different textures of fabrics that appear to be the same colour in daylight, may vary in different artificial lights because the surfaces respond in disparate ways. A lustrous silk will reflect light and appear to shimmer and shine whereas a knotty chenille or dark serge wool will absorb some light into its rough and undulating finish, and therefore appear darker. So look at swatches of textured fabrics in both day and electric light when selecting matching or contrasting types, or building up tone on tone schemes.

The balance of plain and patterned surfaces in a room is important, a busy wallpaper, floral rug and densely striped upholstery will over-stimulate the eye and make it difficult for someone to settle or rest, whereas a totally bland and featureless room will appear boring and mundane. The aim is to find a harmonious middle ground that provides the right ambience.

It can sometimes work to mix floral patterns and geometric prints or weaves but you will need to keep the colour scheme simple and the mix balanced with plains. For example a subtly striped, tone on tone wallpaper can be an effective foil to a large floral design and a self-striped upholstery fabric can work with a subtle floral patterned rug, but this mix needs to be carefully gauged and is something to try out on a mood board (see chapter 7).

As with placing furniture in a space, look carefully at the shapes of the patterns you intend to use. If you put lots of bold stripes with angular furniture one will accentuate the other and the scheme will appear very linear and even sharp. Putting too many polka dot or spot fabrics with rounded furniture will also exaggerate the overall perception of roundness.

Texture is not just a visual element, it is also a tactile part of any decorating scheme. A home should be a place where all the senses are catered for, from the smell of fresh flowers and scented

ABOVE
Tonal (light and dark) printed wallpaper and upholstery fabrics can work well together because the overall impression of colour is similar rather than complimentary or opposing.

FACING PAGE
This muted palette of grey, white and lavender is given added interest with printed and textural pattern.

candles, to the sight of pleasing colours and the feeling of surfaces that touch the skin. The cool smoothness of marble, the soft lushness of silk velvet and the warm cosiness of wool felt will all contribute to the overall enjoyment of a room.

Decorative fabrics don't need to be used in great quantity, especially if they are expensive, just a throw or a few cushion can bring that impression of softness and comfort. It can also be fun and add a contrasting or unexpected texture, perhaps a knobbly tweed cushion amongst the silk and satins, a velvet border around a linen curtain or cashmere throw over a leather chair. This technique is about building up layers of contrast and diversity.

In a family home where large sofas are regularly used for lounging and sitting, and sometimes as a child's trampoline, it is advisable to dress them with removable and washable covers made

ABOVE
Plain coloured upholstery can be made more interesting with contrasting trims, piping or quilting and padding techniques.

FACING PAGE
Surface texture may not at first be obvious to the eye, but it adds a tactile dimension to a scheme which gives another layer of interest.

The colours of the striped wallpaper are repeated in the floral pattern on the seat cushion while just two of the shades are highlighted in the back cushion, this shows how a variety of patterns and designs can be successfully brought together.

Natural materials such as wood and clay bricks also come in a range of colours. When putting down a wood floor choose a shade that compliments the rest of the room, or you can stain or paint an existing wooden floor to a more suitable colour.

in hardwearing materials, especially if you opt for a pale shade. In this case texture may represent durability, but it is worth noting that deep pile or thickly woven fabric surfaces are prone to the accumulation of grime and crumbs, so will need to be regularly wiped and vacuumed to avoid a build up.

Pattern, even if subtle, will also help to disguise any marks or stains that do occur. With pale colours, treat the fabric surface with a repellent finish which will enable most marks to be easily wiped away.

Texture applies not only to fabrics, but also to natural materials such as wood and stone, and in more contemporary settings, the quasi-industrial materials such as concrete, glass and rubber.

Wood can be distressed to appear weathered and bleached for a rustic look or polished and varnished to a high shine for a more sophisticated appearance. It can also be oiled to retain its natural

beauty, but with a light layer of protection, or dyed with a variety of products from imitation wood tones to decorative colours. Oiled wood is often used on kitchen worktops, but it needs to be re-oiled regularly with Danish or linseed oil to maintain the surface durability.

Wood can also be colour washed with a solution of emulsion paint so that the growth lines and grain become more noticeable and prominent, white or off white shades are popular on the floors of coastal or summer houses. And wood can be laid in different designs, as in parquet flooring, so that it creates patterns such as herringbone, chevron, basket and brick, the patterns can also be made more elaborate by using different coloured woods such as pale pine, red cherry and dark mahogany.

ABOVE
Concrete used to be a material found on the outside of modern buildings, but it is increasingly popular indoors. Here the varying shades of the material can be seen in the wall finish.

FACING PAGE
Recycled wood often has an aged or weathered appearance, but this appearance can be replicated with a soft wash of stain or paint over the surface of new timber.

EXPERT ADVICE

Pierre Frey, Paris, London and New York
www.pierrefrey.com

" When it comes to decorating a room pattern and texture are perfect partners; they compliment and highlight each other's charms and personality. A flat surface print needs the texture of a weave to accentuate its qualities and a plain coloured weave will provide the balance to an exotic print, and vice versa, both bringing out the best features in one another. Some might say that pattern and texture follow the rule that opposites attract.

Fabrics can be used to evoke the sense and taste of a country's culture, for example rich jacquards in ethnic motifs, embroided silks and striped fabrics in Indian pink, chilli red, sand yellow and spice shades such as cinnamon and paprika could be used to evoke the idea of a caravan travelling across the lands of the Middle East and Central Asia.

Prints can be a reminder of a time in history, for example a toile du Jouy can tell the story of Napoleon's adventure in Egypt while a Pin Up, monochrome print that pays homage to an Italian holiday poster from the 1950's will conjure up another set of images and ideas.

Weaves and prints are also part of our culture. In Northern Europe and America we favour printed fabrics, often based on the designs imported during the 17th and 18th centuries from India and the Far East. The rise in the fashion of printed fabrics owes much to the Industrial Revolution of the Victorian age which played an enormous part in the development of the of the cotton mills in England. This mechanised printing led to the wider availability of patterned cloths.

Whereas in Eastern Europe and Asia prints are rarely sold, in these cultures woven fabrics are more highly prized, with an emphasis on bright colours and a mix of rich silks and gold yarns. And now with modern technology there is the development of more adaptable and hardwearing material that suits the modern lifestyle. **"**

Similarly stone may be used in its natural, matt form or polished to a glossy surface. With stone such as marble and granite polishing and sealing the surface will highlight the varying colours in its composition and also the shiny elements such as mica and quartz which give the metallic-like flecks that add to its glamour and richness.

Materials used in contemporary design such as concrete and rubber also come in a variety of textures and surface finishes. Concrete can be poured and smoothed so that the surface is flat and even, it can also be polished to a shine or, whilst in the tacky stage, textured or patterned. Templates, such as planks of wood or squares of hessian or a coarsely woven sacking can be gently pressed into the surface and removed leaving an impression of the grain or material that will remain when the concrete sets.

ABOVE
Exposed brickwork can be used to make a focal point of a feature in a room, but its rough uneven surface should be balanced with soft finishes and complimentary colours.

FACING PAGE
Stone is a popular surface finish in bathrooms and showers because it is durable and non-absorbent, the stone can be left mat and plain or polished to a high gloss which can bring out the texture and pattern, especially in marble.

Popular for family kitchens is liquid latex flooring that can be poured on to a pre-prepared smooth surface. It will set with a delicate sheen and is slightly soft underfoot, but is easy to clean and durable. There are also smooth rubber tiles and rolls of rubber flooring that are equally hardwearing and useful in bathrooms, high use hallways and playrooms. And from the realms of industry there are the high-resistance rubber surfaces, some with raised circles or discs patterns, which can be used to bring interest and texture to a single coloured bathroom scheme.

ABOVE
This colourful lino floor brings a splash of colour to the bathroom, but is also practical as it is waterproof and hardwearing.

FACING PAGE
Pale stone or concrete floors are ideal for areas that open out onto gardens, because they won't be affected by muddy boots or grubby pets, but under-floor heating will make it a more convivial finish when the space is being used for relaxing.

Mood Boards and Budgets

Gather samples of materials and review your budget

PRINCIPLE 7

Mood Boards and Budgets

Having done the groundwork assessing the space, defining its use, finding a style and sorting through colours and textures, it is time to amass all the information and make some decisions. Professional designers and decorators use something called a *mood board*; this is a sheet of plain white card or ideally a white-faced notice board on which inspirational pictures and swatches can be pinned.

You will need to gather together photographs of chairs and light fittings taken from catalogues or printed off websites, fabric swatches, and samples of paint colour, wall papers and upholstery materials. And don't forget the details, the trims, braids and tie backs, they are all component parts of the final scheme.

Have a separate mood board for each room you are decorating and assemble all the relevant material beside it. Start by placing the picture of the item of furniture next to the proposed upholstery fabric. When it comes to the size of the pieces of fabric you pin on the *mood board* try to calculate it in proportion to the scale of how it will eventually be used.

For example if you plan floor to ceiling curtains for a pair of large windows, then put up a large swatch of the material you have selected. If you are using a small amount of a woven fabric on the seats of wooden dining chairs, put a smaller piece of fabric on the board. This will give you an overall idea of the balance of colour and texture.

Rather than paint colour directly on to the board, create a sample-size paint swatch on a piece of paper that can be pinned to the board or removed. The idea is that the board is a place where you try and test things until you have the right combination, nothing should be fixed permanently until you are absolutely certain that the scheme is finalised.

You may find that looking at the balance of pattern and plain, primary and tertiary colours that you will need to swap things around. Perhaps the material you had thought was ideal for the seat covers would be better as the curtain fabric or vice versa. This 'playing around' is the fine-tuning process and a vital part of creating a successful scheme.

Once you are happy with the basic appearance of your board, it is

ABOVE
Sometimes a perfect match of paper and fabric can be too much of a good thing. A similar or darker or brighter option may work better, but you can only find out by testing the various options one against the other.

FACING PAGE
Gather together pictures, swatches and samples of things that you like and that inspire you, then mix and match them until you feel you have the right balance of plain and patterned, textured and smooth, light and dark.

Try things together to check if they work: then ask yourself questions for example, Does that shade of blue work with the yellow, Will the brown cushion I already have work with the new yellow and white curtain fabric I've found?

Denim is a fabric more often associated with clothing but it can also be used in interiors, sometimes an unexpected element can bring a new and exciting twist to a scheme.

time to work out how much the scheme will cost. Check the number of metres or yards of fabric needed for the larger areas such as curtains or blinds, and if you are having furniture upholstered in a special heavier weight material then cost that too. Calculate the prices of all the elements such as wallpaper, paint, carpets, underlay, etc. and estimate the costs for making-up, labour and, if necessary, transport. If this is within your budget then you are fine, if it is too high you will need to look back over your choices and see where savings can be made.

You may be able to source similar but cheaper materials by searching on the internet or waiting for the sales, or you may need to focus on one or two special items and replace some more costly items with less expensive ones. This trading is widely done in design, we tend to start with the ultimate range of furnishings and then trim a little here and there and substitute or search for an

ABOVE
A simple and inexpensive scheme can often be lifted by interesting accessories such as old baskets and vintage china; it is better to start plain and within your budget than to overspend and leave other rooms undecorated.

FACING PAGE
Sometime a quantity of something can make a good backdrop, rather than one single expensive glass bottle, a dozen cheaper ones grouped together will make a more striking visual impact.

EXPERT ADVICE

Tara Bernerd of Target Living, London
http://tarabernerd.com/blog/
www.targetliving.com

❝ Design is a process and although attributed to the creative it is also about organisation and a set of guidelines. Indeed adhering to these is essential if you are to keep on target. Try to be decisive and commit to a plan because this is the surest way of staying within a budget, the fatal mistake that many people make is to change ideas half way through or worse to start without a plan and literally design as you go along.

To help with decision making and as an exercise to ensure you don't look back and say: "I wish I had seen that..." make sure you do your research. There are numerous ways to approach this; first stock up on design magazines, collect tear sheets of the latest product, interesting features and/or inspirational interiors. I have also found taking time to visit leading stores and seeing examples of furniture is invaluable; see as much as possible when gathering ideas.

Collecting material samples, fabrics etc is always important. This collection of tear sheets, samples etc will go towards assembling what is known in the trade as a Mood Board.

The process of pulling all this information together is best achieved by looking at it in conjunction with the layout and use of your room. Draw up a floor plan of the area, even if there are no major building works, and consider the shape of the space, where furniture might be placed, then look at the specifications and quantities required for flooring etc. This will give you an idea of the cost and thus the exercise of deciding the budget and the style and concept are achieved at the very outset of the project. ❞

alternative version. Sometimes second hand or vintage finds can be useful. By finding a chair and restoring and reupholstering it yourself, you could save almost half the price of one that has been done and sold through a shop.

There is also the time factor, you may not need to buy everything at once and can therefore spread the cost over a couple of months. By starting with the groundwork, decorating the walls, choosing the flooring and the window dressings you can take longer over purchasing or upholstering the furniture and choosing the accessories.

Also factor in the time that things take to order and to be delivered. You may want a new sofa in a particular fabric, but it could take three or four weeks to get the fabric and then another six to eight weeks to do the upholstery, although you may have to pay a deposit the final payment could be up to three months later. In this way you can defer or stagger the amount of money leaving your bank account.

ABOVE
Using a little of a distinctive or highly patterned fabric can go a long way so you need less of it. In this monochrome scheme the plainness of the white wall is offset by the ornately patterned cover on the chair and the printed curtain.

FACING PAGE
The floral fabric is an expensive designer product, but has been used sparingly as a deep border on a plain curtain and as the front of a cushion. There are many ways to enjoy the luxury of a special material without blowing your budget.

Focal Points and Features

The focal point is the place to which the eye is drawn

Focal Points and Features

The focal point is the place to which the eye is drawn when you first look around a room; it can be a fireplace and mantle, a large attractive picture or a stunning view through a large window. It is the thing you remember most about a room and is often the point around which furniture is arranged.

For example in a room with a hearth and fireplace, chairs tend to be grouped around it so that those sitting in the chairs look toward the fire. The fireplace may also be further enhanced by hanging a picture or mirror above it and so extending the focus further up the wall.

If you choose to hang a mirror above the fire surround, make sure that the frame of the mirror compliments or is in keeping with the style of fitting below. If the mantelpiece is simple white marble, keep the mirror frame classic and elegant, on the other hand if the fireplace is ornately carved and gilded then the mirror frame can reflect that too. The two should be in keeping rather than contrasting.

The hearth or fireplace has traditionally been the focal point of a living room, from its earliest incarnation as a pile of logs and a flame it has become more and more sophisticated, from an iron basket with coals and embers to a setting framed by a mantle and surround. Nowadays even the most modern flat can have the effect of a real fire with gels and flue free appliances framed like a picture in a steel frame and set into a wall.

If the view from the window in your room is particularly attractive then the chairs and sofas may be arranged to face the window, but it will depend on the space and shape of the room and also its use (see chapters 1 and 3). If you have a particularly interesting chair, perhaps an antique or notable modern design such as Tom Dixon's S chair, Ron Arad's Rover chair or a Le Corbusier recliner, by placing it close to or beside the window you will draw attention to it as well.

The arrangement of chairs and sofas should be done in such a way as to be inviting, to bring someone in to the centre of the group or gathering. Avoid long lines of seats that will make the space feel like a waiting room. If the room is difficult to furnish because there

ABOVE
A good frame helps to make a picture the focus of a room. The classic surround to a grand portrait is a deep gilded frame, but smaller pictures can be made larger and more important with a mount of plain or coloured card and a dramatic black frame.

FACING PAGE
Alignment is important. Here, by centering the table and ceiling light so that they are exactly between the windows, a strong focal point to the room has been created.

A number of components bring the eye to this part of the room - the pale wood cabinet contrasts dramatically with the grey wall, the rug is the only area of pattern, and centered on it and directly in front of the cabinet is the vividly upholstered chaise longue. It's a scenario that you couldn't fail to notice.

The bright colour and striking image of the painting makes the chimney breast and fireplace the focal point of this room.

are two or more doors opening into it then try combinations of L-shaped sofas and single chairs arranged so that they neither impede the visual or physical access to and from the doors. And if the focal point is the view, don't put high back chairs immediately in front of the window leave the space free so that the eye has an uninterrupted outlook.

Your room may lack an obvious or existing focal point such as a fireplace but you can create the impression of one by hanging a mirror or good sized, colourful painting on the wall, or with a shelf or bookcase on which a few interesting and carefully selected items are arranged.

Another arrangement that can be used as a focal point is a grouping of four black and white photographs surrounded by black frames; these can look impressive on a plain white wall. Focusing a down-lighter or task light on the artwork will also attract attention to this area and grouping at night.

ABOVE
A group of similar objects such as these round mirrors can make an attractive feature in a hallway or entrance lobby.

FACING PAGE
Wall-mounted shelves provide an ideal support for photographs and pictures, and allow them to be changed and moved without damage to the wall surface.

EXPERT ADVICE

Tim Gosling BIDA, furniture designer and MD of Gosling,
London www.gosling.com

❝ When creating or highlighting features or a focal point
in a room I start by assessing and understanding the
architecture of the place. This involves finding out during
which period it was built and what was fashionable in the
world of architecture at that time.

For example my home was built in 1787 when Robert
Adam was creating designs inspired by Ancient Rome and
the Grand Tour of Europe and the Middle East undertaken
by young gentlemen of that period, all of which had a
huge impact on the style and decoration of houses built in
the eighteenth century.

From the wealth of decorative references I chose to
feature the cornice plasterwork in the study and sitting
room by gilding it and adding a decorative frieze below. I
also included a pair of six foot plaster pillars to
accentuate the feeling of height, and to frame the
panelled doorways and make them a feature of the room.

I feel strongly that symmetry is important because it
creates a strong sense of balance, it can also be used
create a border or edge to a fireplace, doorway or
window, therefore making that area a feature of the room.
Proportion is also a major consideration in my work –
there are set heights for chairs, dining tables, sofas etc
but it is interesting when you play with the scale and size
you are using to create a different drama. Quality is
another key ingredient, especially if the object or piece of
furniture is a focal point or feature of the room. ❞

Another device that contemporary designers use is a pair of parallel shelves on which pictures can be arranged rather than hung directly on the wall. The pictures may vary in size and can overlap, but as they rest on a shelf they can be easily rearranged or changed to update or alter the emphasis without leaving marks or nail holes on the wall.

In modern apartments where the walls tend to be mainly of glass it can be difficult to find a space on which to hang a picture or fix a shelf, so you may turn your attention to a piece of free standing sculpture to draw the eye, and keep the focus in the room rather than drifting out to the views beyond.

A good size piece of sculpture, whether in metal, wood or stone, may be placed directly in front of a window because in a room with two or three glass walls the view can be seen from other aspects of the room, but don't obscure all the windows, leave at least half of the space clear.

The focal point doesn't always have to be on a wall. In a large room you can bring visual attention to an area with a rug or mat

ABOVE
Although the painting on the wall is a focal point, its prominence is enhanced and amplified by the arrangement of the low sideboard underneath and the matching pair of chairs, one on either side.

FACING PAGE
To ensure that the colour and texture of the painting over the fireplace is the focal point in this room, the contents of the cupboards on either side have been screened with curtains of a neutral fabric.

around which sofas and chairs are arranged, and again lighting can be used to focus awareness on that part of the space.

Other features in a room may include architectural mouldings or friezes, architraves and panelled doors, all of which can be highlighted to bring character and interest to the scheme. They can also be decorated in a way that will enhance or further emphasise the focal point of the room. For example if the focal point of the room is an elegant pale grey marble fireplace and the chimney breast above it, and the walls in the rest of the room are decorated in a rich Prussian blue, by painting the skirting boards and cornice in a greyish white shade the parallel borders at the top and bottom of the wall will draw the eye towards the fireplace.

If the windows of a room with a view are framed by panelled shutters rather than curtains, the inset panels could be painted a darker or lighter tone than the rest of the shutter, giving a feeling of depth and interest without distracting from the scene through the

window. If you choose to use curtains and a pelmet around such a window this will also create a frame, but the curtains should be tied back so as not to encroach on the view and the pelmet should frame but not overpower the top of the window.

In an ornately styled period room, the finer details of the ceiling centre rose and decorative cornice plaster work could be picked out in gold leaf which may echo the gilt frame of the mirrors and pictures elsewhere in the room. In cases like this, you need to ensure that the plasterwork is of sufficient quality and in good repair, and also that the gilding is subtle rather than overpowering because you won't want to make the focus of attention the ceiling.

ABOVE
Although this decorative table by Oriel Harwood is eye-catching in its own right, the addition of the tall candlestick doubles the overall effect, because as you walk into the room the candlestick is at eye level, whereas the table is below.

FACING PAGE
Sometimes just one dramatic piece of art or sculpture is all a room needs, the contrast between this ornate, coral inspired white mirror frame and the dark, mossy green walls make an instant impact.

PRINCIPLE 9
Display and Storage

Display and storage can be one in the same thing

PRINCIPLE 9

Display and Storage

Display and storage can be one in the same thing because, in some instances, the two objectives become one. In a dining room a shelf of sparkling wine glasses will be an attractive part of the décor, but will also provide a practical way in which to contain and store them. In the kitchen a dresser or plate rack may be used to present a collection of china or tableware, but it also means that the pieces are easily accessible and ready for use.

The areas where items are arranged and displayed can be decorated to enhance the things on show. For example a collection of blue and white willow pattern china would look impressive if displayed against a background painted in a lighter hue of the blue in the design, rather than against a cream or other coloured background which may dilute the impact of the blue.

Plain white or black shelves will bring unity and cohesion to a diverse display of objects in differing colours and patterns, and collections of coloured glass vases and bowls look effective when arranged on glass shelves, especially if the shelves are lit with LED or task lights so that the glass appears to glow.

Attractive items that are not often used, and may therefore gather dust, should be stored and displayed in glass fronted cabinets or cupboards. Some metal and silverwares are prone to tarnish, but if kept in tightly closed units the discolouration process may be delayed. Fragile objects are also safer kept behind a glass fronted door, because they are less likely to be picked up or knocked over.

The key to successful display is grouping, as it affects the way in which objects are viewed. In design terms it is stated that odd numbers are more interesting than even, so groups of three, five or seven smaller objects are preferable two or fours. Also try to arrange objects of varying sizes so that the eye is taken up to a specific high point. You can also layer displays so that larger darker pieces are in the background and smaller lighter coloured objects are in front. Or on deep bookshelves, books maybe arranged to the back while the remaining space at the front of the shelf can be used for photographs and trinkets.

In modern minimalist rooms you may want to keep objects to a

ABOVE
Glass and crystal objects are attractive because they don't contribute bulk to an arrangement, but they catch the light and glisten and sparkle attractively.

FACING PAGE
Storage doesn't need to be dull, here a row of small gilded drawers makes an attractive feature in a dressing room.

**This Home Office storage has been
designed so that some areas are left
open for easy access and ordered
display while other areas are
concealed so that clutter and
unattractive files can be kept out
of sight.**

**Architectural shelving and well
organised books show how display
can be an integral part of an overall
design scheme.**

ABOVE
The space under a staircase is often wasted, but this window seat not only provides somewhere to sit, the base also contains two deep storage drawers.

FACING PAGE
A disused chimney breast can be recycled to accommodate a set of recessed shelves. The wood surround of this shelving unit acts as a contrast to the plain white of the walls and visually frames the objects within.

few well chosen pieces. There is an oriental custom whereby the household's precious artefacts and possessions are stored in a chest beneath a niche in the wall. Each item is taken out in turn and displayed alone in the niche so that its full beauty can be admired, without the distraction of other items. In an area of display like this the item on show must be of high quality and real interest because there is little else to draw attention away from it.

You can highlight and define a specific or special object by placing it on a mat or coloured base. For example, a small group of fine white porcelain vases may be lost if placed on a glass top table in a pale coloured room, but by placing them on a red or vibrant

coloured mat they will be framed and contained thereby becoming more noticeable.

Transparent objects such as glass benefit from being placed against a background or on a base of a different colour and in some cases mirror can be effective as it reflects the object as well as the available natural light, so giving the glass its own highlight.

Lighting is a useful tool when it comes to displaying objects and especially when a dark object is placed against a wall in a deep colour. Glass and china as well as paintings and artworks can be illuminated by individual electrical task lights which focus the beam and thus the eye, on the object.

Anything that is arranged or displayed in a room must be kept in pristine condition, therefore frequently washed and polished, and displays don't have to be static. When returning objects from their regular wash or polish try putting them in a different position or

ABOVE
Pictures don't always have to be hung in regimented rows; here a random arrangement of different sized prints and objects forms a patchwork-like image on the wall.

FACING PAGE
Decorative art glass is best displayed with space around it, so that each piece can be seen from a different angle and admired in its own right. Lighting, whether natural or a specific spot light, will help to bring out the glass's inherent beauty and colour.

EXPERT ADVICE

Robert and Cortney Novogratz of The Novogratz,
Designers and TV hosts, New York
www.thenovogratz.com

" Storage is always an important part of any interior
project we are involved in because clutter is the enemy of
a well-designed, functional and chic environment.

There should always be a place to stow the things you
absolutely need, where they can be accessed easily but
are clear of your living space. Once clutter is banished,
your room will immediately feel more spacious and look
sleeker. We are big proponents of paring down belong-
ings, creating great storage systems in our closets, and
putting small items like toys etc. into cabinets where the
kids can reach them easily, to take out when they need
them and put away when they are done!

Regarding display, accessories and art are certainly a
large part of any stylish interior décor. We love to find
new and exciting art to showcase in our design projects,
and in art we include photography, painting and
sculpture, multi-media.

Whether from established or emerging artists from
around the globe, art can give instant and very powerful
flavour to your space. The same with accessories—they
can be a source of colour, a vintage piece that functions
as the focal point of a room, or something whimsical that
makes your home unique. "

ABOVE
A mirror has been placed behind the shelves in this hallway and acts not only to reflect the light, but also to allow people to see all the way around the small objects that are displayed there, without having to pick them up.

FACING PAGE
Shelving systems can be attractive in their own right. Here the objects are comparatively plain, but the unusual ladder and plank support adds to their interest.

group, this will refresh the appearance of the room and will bring attention to a different object or trinket.

Having said that objects are best displayed in odd numbers, this rule is often ignored when it comes to furniture, where matching pairs are much sought after. For example two identical console tables on either side of a fire place, or a couple of decorative Rococo chairs, lined up like sentries on either side of a doorway lend a certain formality and balance to a scheme.

Displaying pictures and photographs is an art in itself. Grouping small, similarly sized pictures together can be more effective and pleasing on the eye than a couple of single pictures dotted along a vast expanse of wall. In general pictures should be hung so that the centre of the image is at eye level and also similar subject or colour themes should be arranged together, so a collection of landscape pictures or several pen and ink drawings.

Storage is a very important feature of the home but, especially

LEFT
Opaque or frosted glass can be used to camouflage the contents of a cupboard where solid doors might feel appear heavy or bulky.

FACING PAGE
Some storage benefits from being featureless; this recessed wardrobe is made almost invisible by having its doors covered in the same wallpaper as the rest of the room.

for unattractive objects, storage like this is at its best and most effective when unseen. Bulky files, winter jumpers and spare duvets should be kept in cupboards with solid doors or in zipped bags under the bed and concealed by a valance.

Small and unattractive items can be stored in boxes, the boxes may be simple and stylish and therefore left on display, while the clutter or stuff inside is shielded from view.

Bulky fabric items, such as a winter headboard cover and valance, summer curtains or seasonally changed cushion covers can be stored in vacuum bags. These thick plastic bags have a valve mechanism on the top and once the fabrics and covers are zipped inside the excess air is squeezed or sucked out with a vacuum cleaner attachment, so that the bulk is considerably reduced.

ABOVE
Even everyday kitchenware can be attractive when well displayed. Objects that are used regularly are often best stored on open shelves so that they are easily accessible.

FACING PAGE
This book-lined staircase is a useful way of creating an accessible library and utilising a difficult space. The lighting detail also adds to the appearance of the arrangement.

To guard against stored clothes and fabrics being damaged by moths, place moth repellent cedar wood or camphor balls amongst them and make sure that everything is clean before being packed away, so that there are no spills or food marks to attract the insects.

Accessorising

Accessories are the finishing touches to a room

PRINCIPLE 10

Accessorising

Accessories are the finishing touches to a room and include the light, moveable pieces such as cushions and throws, loose chair covers, lampshades, vases and artefacts as well as less weighty curtains.

These soft furnishings are often used to bring highlight or accent colours and a variety of textures to a scheme and can also be a way of using a special or expensive fabric in a small and affordable quantity. For example you could use a small amount of a costly hand woven, patterned silk on the face of a cushion while making the back in plain, basic cotton. Or use a standard, unfussy fabric for the body of a curtain but add a border and pelmet of a contrasting or co-ordinating jacquard.

In recent times there has been a growing trend for bringing a seasonal update to a room by changing the accessories. This maybe because soft furnishings have becomes less expensive and easier to buy; also having two sets of covers spreads the wear and tear on the materials and leaves one change free for repairs and laundering while the other is in use.

To bring about summer/winter or spring/autumn change choose a muted or neutral scheme for the larger, fixed pieces of up-holstered furniture and the main wall colour. Then select a basic 'family' colour that will work across a wide range of patterns and fabrics. Finally, work out light and dark palettes on which to focus each of the two contrasting seasonal looks.

For the winter you may have heavyweight curtains in bottle green velvet but in the summer swap them for light, minty green voiles. Cushion covers for the winter scheme may be in ochre and gold shades of knobbly chenille and comforting brown and orange felt and fleece, whereas in the summer they are in fresh, citrus shades of linen and cotton.

Upright dining chairs with washable, cotton tab-tied or slip-on tabard covers offer some protection against regular family use, but can also be part of the seasonal scheme. The covers could be in fresh beige linen or cream cotton for the sunnier season and subtly ribbed, cocoa coloured corduroy for the autumn. If you can't afford a whole different scheme, or don't have enough space to store the

ABOVE
This brightly striped rug brings pattern and colour to an all white room, but could be easily swapped for one in richer, more jewel-like colours for a seasonal change.

FACING PAGE
Accessories can be used to bring contrast, texture and tactile qualities to a room scheme.

ABOVE
This collection of red glass picks up on the single red line in the artwork hanging on the wall. The glass also brings a block of colour in to the centre of an otherwise monochrome scheme.

FACING PAGE
If your window looks out over a boring or unattractive view, a collection of glass will bring colour and interest to the window are without blocking the light.

soft furnishings when they are not being used, you could try reversible cushion covers and tab-top or pole hung curtains so that when the time comes you simply turn them around for a different colour way.

Glass and china are made in a myriad of colours so there is always a good chance of finding a piece or pieces that perfectly match your scheme, no matter how unusual and off-beat your choice of colours might be.

Arrangements of colourful china and glass will increase the visual stimulus in your room and can be used to reinforce highlighted or accent colours. For example in a mainly grey sitting room a vase or collection of ceramic bowls in a primary colour will be a focus of attention. On a shelf against a beige wall a group of highly decorated and gilded china figures or vessels will be noticeable, but arrangements must be limited and well displayed (see chapter 9) otherwise your room may take on the appearance of a junk shop.

Accessories can help to transform a plain room, here a velvet padded headboard is used as a backdrop for coat hangers, and the ornate gilded mirror beside the bath and the wall light with glass drops add a feeling or richness and luxury.

EXPERT ADVICE

Romeo Sozzi, CEO and the designer of Promemoria
Promemoria, Leeco, Milan, London, Paris, New York and
Moscow www.promemoria.com

" My intention is to create an atmosphere where one can
feel comfortable and serene and where it is possible to
find one's own place within. Accessories are often more
important than the pieces of furniture themselves
because they reveal one's personality.

   The details, for example handles, can be like
sculptures, can be made of bronze or Murano glass which
create reflective light effects and are tactile and
interesting when in contact with the hand. These small
details remind us of the craftsmanship and skill that are
an important part of the creative and manufacturing
process. The same applies to walls covered with leather,
and with the choice of the wood for the floor, the detail
and quality will all contribute to the overall pleasure and
enjoyment of the room.

   Well finished furniture must embody all the essential
qualities: comfort, originality and harmony. Accessorising
doesn't come only from desires but also from dreams. **"**

Many people prefer not to hang paintings or mirrors above the
head of their bed, but a decorative bed head, a canopy or hanging
can be used as an accessory to brighten up an otherwise plain
room. Removable bed head covers are another area where seasonal
colour and pattern can be used, with a rich warm coloured cover for
the winter months and a lighter, fresher colour for spring and
summer. A matching valance, the skirt of fabric that covers the base
and legs of bed, will also help to complete the scheme.

A valance maybe a relatively small amount of colour but it can
help to ground a scheme. For example, by putting a dark valance at
the bottom of a bed dressed in white or pale coloured linen you
make the bed appear more solid and set on the floor.

A counterpane or throw is a useful accessory and will help to
break up a large expanse of white or plain bed linen, especially on a
double or king-size bed that dominates a room. Bedside mats or
rugs are small accessories, but in a bedroom with a wooden floor
they will provide not only a soft and warm place on which to put

In this opulent, loosely Indian themed bedroom sari silk used as curtains and voiles; the colour of the lighter voile curtains gives the daylight a sunny yellow cast. Inexpensive painted silk pictures have also been framed and hung in a row between the windows.

your feet when getting in and out of bed, but also another opportunity to add a splash of colour.

In a bathroom towels are the most versatile accessory, if the bath and background tiles are white or a single colour then towels in a primary or contrasting shade can be an important feature. For example black towels in a predominantly white and chrome bathroom will look very striking, while in a pale blue bathroom towels and bathmats in dark blue could be used to enhance the cool, fresh element of the scheme.

ABOVE
Pottery and china comes in a myriad of shades and can be grouped to highlight a range of colours in a rug, curtain fabric or cushion cover.

FACING PAGE
The monochrome rug and black edged cushions bring an element of pattern and interest to this otherwise plainly furnished room.

Checklists

Get yourself a dedicated notebook...

Checklists

Introduction

Before you start do your research and gather ideas:

1. Get yourself a dedicated notebook and file or folder in which you can note the relevant measurements of the room you are decorating, the budget you are aiming for and amass bills, estimates and colour and fabric swatches, etc.

2. Measure your room, especially windows if you are having curtains or blinds made. Make sure you have the correct measurements from where the curtain pole or track might go, and the drop to the sill or floor, depending on what length you wish to have.

3. Make a note of the unusual features such as radiators or doorway openings that might affect the pull back of a curtain or the size of a rug or carpet. For example, if the pile of the rug is thick it may not fit under the door so you may want the rug to finish short of the doorway, or the base of the door may have to be reduced so that it can slide over the carpet.

4. Look through magazines, books and brochures for ideas and make photocopies, or where possible, tear out pages of styles, furniture, colours and textiles that you like. Put these in a file or box.

5. Visit shops and stores, talk to people in the shops about the period or style of the furniture or fabric they stock, sometimes finding out about the designer or maker can help you get an idea of where the inspiration or look of the product comes from which in turn can help with deciding on a theme or scheme.

Principle 1: Purpose and Function

1. How often will you use this room and at what time of the day will it be most used (e.g., every day, evenings only, once a week)?

2. Who will be using the room (e.g., children, homeworker)?

3. Is the room a formal space where you might entertain guests and will this affect the style and appearance?

4. Does the room have more than one function (living room and office)? Are these one in the same or do the functions need to be separate?

5. Is the room a passage way to other parts of the house or apartment or is it connected to another room, (e.g., an en-suite bathroom to a main bedroom or a kitchen to a dining area)?

Principle 2: Style

1. Do you have a particular era that you would like to emulate (e.g., art deco)?

2. Is your furniture of a particular period or does it lend itself to a particular style?

3. Do you prefer an eclectic look or one that follows a consistent scheme?

4. Is there an object (painting, sculpture, piece of furniture) that defines or inspires the way you want your living space to look?

5. Do people who will be sharing the space have differing views on décor?

Principle 3: Space and Shape

1. How big is the space you want to decorate?

2. If it is a small space, do you want to make it look larger?

3. If is a large space, do you want it to be more cozy or to create smaller spaces within the larger space?

4. How will you use your existing furniture? Do you need to get rid of some pieces and replace them with new ones?

5. If the room has an unusual shape (e.g., a rounded wall) how can the space be used effectively?

Principle 4: Light

1. How much natural light does the room get? Are there times of day when the sunlight is too strong or when there is little natural light?

2. If the room has minimal natural light, does its function mean that it will need a lot of artificial light (e.g., office or kitchen) or can it have softer light (e.g., bedroom)?

3. If the room serves more than one function (e.g., kitchen/dining room) will you need to plan lighting that will accommodate both brighter and dimmer lighting?

4. What type of lighting or lighting combination do you want in each room (e.g., ceiling lights, table lamps, floor lamps)?

5. Do you want to highlight certain objects in the room such as a painting or a chimney breast?

Principle 5: Colour

1. How will the room be used? Would bright stimulating colours or more restful shades be appropriate or would a neutral palette give you more scope to add bright accessories and furniture?

2. If your decoration scheme is following a particular period are there colour palettes that are relevant to the decoration of that time that will help you to capture the mood?

3. Is the space to be decorated dark or small? If so, consider using light colours to make it appear brighter and larger, or do you want to make the room cosy and snug, in that case look at the warmer, redder palette and deeper richer colours.

4. Do you or does anyone sharing the space have a favourite colour that could be the basis of the colour scheme?

5. Are there particular objects or pieces of furniture that would influence the colour chosen? For example, a contemporary artwork with strong colours might look best on a white wall or against a background of a pale hue of one of the colours featured in the painting.

6. How do you plan to mix different colours in a room? Will you opt for tones of the same colour, pick out highlights in complementary shades or will you go for a dramatic monochromatic scheme?

7. Look at the Colour Wheel as a reference for colours that are in a 'family' and those that contrast.

8. Are you planning to change your accessory colour palette according to the season, if so look at groups of colours that offer a definite contrast – a cool or fresh scheme for the summer and a warm and comforting palette for the winter.

Principle 6: Pattern and Texture

1. What types of textures work well together? Think of contrast and tactile qualities.

2. Do you want to create a crisp or lustrous effect with your furnishings or a comfy informal effect, for example?

3. What kind of use will the room get? Is it a family room where the furniture may get lots of wear and tear? If so look at durable fabrics with protective finishes.

4. If you are using more than one pattern, do they complement each other or does the room look too 'busy'? Try and find a balance so that the scheme is not overly fussy.

5. Adding pattern to a plain white room provides more interest and can be done gradually so that the eye becomes accustomed to it without being overwhelmed.

Principle 7: Creating Mood boards and budgets

1. How much money have you budgeted for decoration? Is your budget flexible, are you prepared to delay or wait for something or does everything need to be done at once? If you can delay some things highlight them or put them in a 'wish list' box to one side so that you can add or subtract them as your planning progresses.

2. Have you estimated how much material or paint you will need? And costed it? Also do you need to add transportation or professional fitting charges?

3. Can you source some of what you need more cheaply? What about second hand or vintage items?

4. Do you need to do everything at once or can you redecorate in stages? And, if so, what makes sense to do first?

5. Have you created a mood board of the style and feel of the scheme you are aiming for with pictures from magazines and pieces of fabric or wallpaper that represent part of the look?

6. Have you worked out a schedule for when the work should be completed and in what order?

Principle 8: Focal points and features

1. Are there special features in a room to which you want to draw attention?

2. Are there features you want to hide or draw the eye away from?

3. When someone enters the room, what do you want them to notice first?

4. Have you created visual access to the feature you want to highlight? Is it clearly seen or might it be obscured by, for example, high back chairs in front of a window that is your focus?

5. Could you use lighting to enhance a feature or to draw attention to an object or space?

6. Are there colours that would make a key feature stand out?

Principle 9: Display and storage

1. Could you both store and display objects at the same time such as using a Welsh dresser with decorative china teacups or plates or a shelf of sparkling crystal wine glasses?

2. How can you best enhance the objects you wish to display by the use of lighting or colour?

3. Do you want your storage to be discrete and unobtrusive?

4. Have you grouped items in a harmonious way?

5. Is the storage area one that you will have to access frequently or is it, for example, seasonal storage which may be accessed only a few times per year?

Principle 10: Accessorising

1. If you are adding cushions to a sofa or chair, do they enhance it by adding interesting colour and texture? Or are they plain and used to help lessen the impact of a densely patterned and brightly coloured upholstery fabric?

3. Do you want your accessories to harmonize or contrast with the colour of the walls or other elements of your colour scheme?

4. Have you got the balance right between artfully arranged objects and clutter?

5. Have the objects been arranged or grouped in an interesting way? Could they be made more interesting if put against a different background, on an eye level shelf or broken up in to smaller groups or even grouped together in one larger unit? Play around with them until you get the right combination and position.

Picture Credits

[Every effort has been made to credit the appropriate source, please contact us if you find any errors or omissions so that these may be corrected in any future printings.]

page 92-93 Elisabeth Aarhus/ Mainstreamimages/snoarc.no; 109 Elisabeth Aarhus/Main-streamimages/oddthorsen.no; 147 Elisabeth Aarhus/ Mainstreamimages/avsolortebond epiker.no.

pages 26, 138 Julian Abrams/ Mainstreamimages/Michaelis Boyd Associates.
pages 186 Sue Barr/Main-streamimages/Lynch Architects.
pages 2, 106, 174 Anitta Behrendt/Mainstreamimages.
page 134 Philip Bier/ Mainstreamimages/Nicolas Tye Architects.
pages 91, 189 James Brittain/ Mainstreamimages/Simon Gill Architects.

pages 9, 18-19, 21, 63, 148 Darren Chung/Mainstreamimages/mufti. co.uk; 22, 31, 36, 41, 54, 70, 76, 80, 102, 112, 119, 120, 156, 161, 164, 169, 172, 185, 193, 202-204 Darren Chung/Mainstream-images; 25 Darren Chung/Mainstreamimages/ kitchencoordination.co.uk;, 35 Darren hung/Mainstreamimages/ electriksheep.com; 49 Darren Chung/Mainstreamimages/ haddowpartnership.co.uk; 55 Darren Chung/ Mainstreamimages/ teedinteriors.com; 83, 188 Darren Chung/ Mainstreamimages/michalsky.com; 84, 129 Darren Chung/ Mainstreamimages/timorous-beastiescom; 85 Darren Chung/ Mainstreamimages/annemachin-architects.com; 95 Darren Chung/ Mainstreamimages/roundhouse-design.com; 111, 113 Darren Chung/ Mainstreamimages/shakethesky.c om; 123, 168 Darren Chung/ Mainstreamimages/alacarter.com; 125 Darren Chung/ Mainstreamimages/ lizbulldesign.com; 133 Darren Chung/Mainstreamimages/bobbyo pen.com; 140 Darren Chung/ Mainstreamimages/martinswatto n.com; 141 Darren Chung/Mainstreamimages/w2pro ducts.com; 153 Darren Chung/ Mainstreamimages/the-

englishstudio.com; 178 Darren Chung/Mainstream-images/gregoryphillips.com; 179 Darren Chung/ Mainstreamimages/hipauntie.com; 201 Darren Chung/Mainstream-images/ spratley.co.uk.

pages 72-73 Peter Cook/ Mainstreamimages/Jonathan Ellis-Miller.
page 37 Dennis Gilbert/Main-streamimages/Formwork Architects Ltd.
page 34 Richard Glover/Main-streamimages/Smart Design Studio.

pages 10, 30 Sarah Hogan/Main-streamimages/housela-france.com; 38-39, 146 Sarah Hogan/Mainstreamimages; 45, 166 Sarah Hogan/Mainstream-images /sue williamsacourt.co.uk. page 100 Nick Hulton/Main-streamimages/Jonathan Clark.

pages 6-7 Ray Main/Mainstream-images/stilllife.uk.com; 8, 11, 13, 14-15, 62, 103, 115, 131, 149, 160, 187, 200, 205 Ray Main/Main-streamimages; 12, 27, 69, 77, 110 Ray Main/Mainstreamimages/ fionabarrattinteriors.com; 16, 88 Ray Main/Mainstreamimages/ Foundassociates.com; 32-33 Ray Main/Mainstreamimages/ thehouseat.com; 40 Ray Main/ Mainstreamimages/ Designalacarter.com; 44 Ray Main/Mainstreamimages/gabbert as.com; 46-47 Ray Main/Mainstreamimages/su-shilla.com; 48 Ray Main/Main-streamimages/ Architect Oliver Morgan; 52 Ray Main/Main-streamimages/Arne.Maynard; 53 Ray Main/Mainstream-images/Talismanantiques.com; 56-57, 89, 104 Ray Main/Main-streamimages/domusfurniture.co. uk; 58 Ray Main/ Main-streamimages/ John F Rolf Design and Build; 68 Ray Main/ Main-streamimages/Wilson and Cohone Arch; 71, 192 Ray Main/ Main-streamimages/Jim Thompson.com; Ray Main/Main-streamimages/ cullumnightingale.com; 81 Ray

Main/ Mainstreamimages/ saffroninteriorarts.com; 86-87 Ray Main/ Mainstreamimages/Arch Kralform.com; 90 Ray Main/Mainstreamimages/ julianstair.com; 96, 97 Ray Main/Mainstreamimages/ janconstantine.com; 98 Ray Main/ Mainstreamimages/design echodesign.co.uk; 101 Ray Main/ Mainstreamimages/Artist Cindy Lass; 108 Ray Main/ Mainstreamimages/Designer Rabih Hage; 114 Ray Main/Mainstreamimages/ www.squintlimited.com; Ray Main/Mainstreamimages/StudioO HM.com; 122 Ray Main/Mainstreamimages/ appleyhoare.com; Ray Main/ Mainstreamimages/ ACQ Architects; Ray Main/Mainstreamimages/Osborne & Little; 132, 159, 167 Ray Main/Allegra Hicks Design; 139, 190-191 Ray Main/Mainstreamimages/ atelierabigailahern.com; 142-143, 173 Ray Main/Mainstreamimages/ Taylor Howes Designs Ltd; 145 Ray Main/Mainstreamimages/hoteldup etitmoulin.com; 154-155, 162 Ray Main/Mainstreamimages/tgosling. com; 158 Ray Main/ Mainstreamimages/Susann Eschenfelder; Ray Main/ Mainstreamimages/ Kbjarchitects.co.uk; 170-171, 176 Ray Main/ Mainstreamimages/ domusfurniture.co.uk; 175 Ray Main/Mainstreamimages/ Designer Meltons.co.uk; 177 Ray Main/Mainstreamimages/Arch. Polescuk Architects; 183 Ray Main/Mainstreamimages/designaddi ct.com; 194 Ray Main/ Mainstreamimages/bendelisi. com; 195 Ray Main/Mainstreamimages/ Baileyshomeandgarden.com; 196-197 Ray Main/Mainstream-images/Jura Distillery.

page 43, 99, 107 Paul Massey/ Mainstreamimages
page 152, 157, 182, 184 Paul Raeside/Mainstreamimages
page 23, 59 Edmund Sumner/ Mainstream-images/James Langford Architects; 64-64

Edmund Sumner/Mainstream-images/Waro Kishi; 74 Edmund Sumner/ Mainstreamimages/the Pike Practice; 82 Edward Sumner/ Mainstreamimages/ Foster and Partners/United Designers; 135 Edmund Sumner/Mainstream-images/Sou Fujimoto Architects. 121 James Winspear/Main-streamimages/Consarc.Consulting Architects.

The author would especially like to thank the following people and companies for providing imagery for this book:
page 28 Courtesy of Taylor Howes Designs/www.thdesigns.co.uk.
page 42 National Trust Paint Collection, courtesy of Fired Earth/www.firedearth.com.
page 44 Courtesy of Claudia Zinzan for Shelleece Stanaway Design, Auckland New Zealand.
page 51 Courtesy of Lulu Lytle, Soane Britain/www.soane.co.uk.
page 67 Yabu Pushelberg, courtesy of Beth Cooper Public Relations/ www.yabupushelberg.com.
page 79 Sally Storey, John Cullen Lighting/www.johncullen-lighting.co.uk courtesy of The Ideas Network.
page 104 Courtesy of Jonathan Adler/www.jonathanadler.com.
pages 116-117, 126-127, 136 Courtesy of Pierre Frey Paris/www.pierrefrey.com (photographer: Marie-Pierre Morel).
page 128 This Morning, courtesy of Snow PR/liz@snowpr.com.
page 150 Tara Bernerd, Target Living/www.tarabernerd.com; www.targetliving.com (photographer: Philip Vile)
page 180 Robert and Cortney Novogratz/www.thenovogratz.com courtesy of Carol Leggett Public Relations.
page 198 Romeo Sozzi, Promemoria, courtesy of Conseil Relazioni Pubbliche/ www.promemoria.com.

Illustrations pages 24, 60-61, 94 Keith Lovegrove.

Index